Doing
Relationship-Based
Social Work

of related interest

Relationship-Based Research in Social Work
Understanding Practice Research
Edited by Gillian Ruch and Ilse Julkunen
ISBN 978 1 84905 457 7
eISBN 978 1 78450 112 9

Relationship-Based Social Work
Getting to the Heart of Practice
Edited by Gillian Ruch, Danielle Turney and Adrian Ward
ISBN 978 1 84905 003 6
eISBN 978 0 85700 383 6

Learning from Baby P
The Politics of Blame, Fear and Denial
Sharon Shoesmith
ISBN 978 1 78592 003 5
eISBN 978 1 78450 238 6

Tackling Child Neglect
Research, Policy and Evidence-Based Practice
Edited by Ruth Gardner
Foreword by David Howe
ISBN 978 1 84905 662 5
eISBN 978 1 78450 165 5

Working with Violence and Confrontation
Using Solution Focused Approaches
Creative Practice with Children, Young People and Adults
Judith Milner and Steve Myers
Foreword by Andrew Turnell
ISBN 978 1 78592 055 4
eISBN 978 1 78450 312 3

Mastering Social Work Supervision
Jane Wonnacott
ISBN 978 1 84905 177 4
eISBN 978 0 85700 403 1

DOING RELATIONSHIP-BASED SOCIAL WORK

*A Practical Guide to Building
Relationships and Enabling Change*

Edited by
Mary McColgan and Cheryl McMullin

Jessica Kingsley *Publishers*
London and Philadelphia

First published in 2017
by Jessica Kingsley Publishers
73 Collier Street
London N1 9BE, UK
and
400 Market Street, Suite 400
Philadelphia, PA 19106, USA

www.jkp.com

Library of Congress Cataloging in Publication Data
A CIP catalog record for this book is available from the Library of Congress

British Library Cataloguing in Publication Data
A CIP catalogue record for this book is available from the British Library

ISBN 978 1 78592 014 1
eISBN 978 1 78450 256 0

Printed and bound in the United States

DEDICATION

We would like to dedicate this book to our esteemed colleague John McLaughlin, one of our contributors from Ulster University who very sadly passed away before this book was completed. John embodied the ethos of relationship-based social work with service users, students and colleagues and will be a great loss to the profession. A special note of thanks to Maura O'Connor for ensuring John's contribution was published.

ACKNOWLEDGEMENTS

Editors: We would like to thank all the contributors to the book who gave their time, experience and dedication – without their valuable support the book would not have been possible. We would like to thank service users, students and practitioners who gave their invaluable input into the model.

Mary McColgan: A special thank-you to my children, Aoife and Aodhan, for their love and support throughout the journey we have travelled together. Best feathers in my wing!

Cheryl McMullin: I would like to thank Jo Marley, Director of Bryson Care, for all her support and generosity. Special thanks to Siobhan Wylie and Denise MacDermott for all their support and encouragement. I would like to give a special thank-you to my family, Jim, Alex and Eve McMullin.

CONTENTS

INTRODUCTION

Mary McColgan

Inevitably, the challenge of writing a book about relationships has its genesis in gathering the different perspectives of all the contributors, sharing a common vision about why the book is important, establishing common ground about how the work will be approached and embarking on a journey. The production of this book has reflected this journey because the process of writing and editing has mirrored the reality of building relationships: exploring different professional perspectives, responding to unexpected life challenges, supporting each other and, significantly, coming to terms with the untimely death of our esteemed colleague John McLaughlin. The common denominator for us all was our conviction that building relationships lay at the heart of our work as practitioners and educators and was reflected in our practice with service users, students, colleagues and other professionals, but at the same time articulating how central relationship-building was conflicted with the reality of the challenges faced in working in organisations, teams and in a context of economic austerity and rationing of resources.

The unique aspect of this book is its combined academic and practice emphasis with the blended approach of expertise. This book aims to explore a positive approach to learning and development, highlighting the importance of re-establishing that relationship-based social work and caring is fundamental to best practice. Contemporary studies about service provision in the context of families, children and older people (Hood *et al.* 2016; Ward and Barnes 2016) endorse the significance of relationships as the basis for effective practice.

This book will add to the current published literature of the growing body of professionals and academics promoting relationship-based practice such as Trevithick, Hennessey, Cooper, Megele, Winter and Ruch. We would like to bring the voice of the service user to the forefront and it offers practitioners a 4 Stage Relationship Model underpinned by evidence and theory specific to the relationship-building process which is unique and can be easily applied to practice.

The book will give consideration to the challenges posed by working within a context of austerity and structural inequalities such as poverty, discrimination and political and economic tensions for service delivery. Relationships and communication are the foundation of good social work practice highlighted in the national and international literature. However, social work practice is coming under increased scrutiny in the current socio-political climate. It is crucial that the book takes cognisance of this but it will offer the reader a reassuring and refreshing approach to practice.

The model of building relationships in social work outlined in Chapter 1 informs each of the chapters and explains why the relationship is important at each phase of the social work process. The approach is underpinned with knowledge of motivational interviewing techniques, strengths-focused practice resilience, emotional intelligence and empowerment. The model is to some extent mirroring the social work process of engagement, assessment, intervention and evaluation/termination.

This book will be informative and practical for a broad range of readers, from social work students to practitioners and professionals. Its aim is to cover a wide range of themes under the umbrella of relationships experienced within the social work context. This will offer a practical guide and will help navigate the complex interaction and subtle issues that arise through the relationship-building process. The first chapter gives an overview of relationship-based practice and introduces the model. Chapter 2 defines the broader historical, social and political landscape which has shaped the backdrop for relationship-based practice. McLaughlin contends that, although the commitment to relationship-based practice has been subordinated to the interests of neoliberalism and managerialism, research evidence supports the centrality of relationships in work with vulnerable adults and their carers. In extrapolating the argument for the benefits of relationship-based work, McLaughlin advocates a holistic approach as the basis for empowering service users and carers.

In Chapter 3, Marshall explores the challenges posed in utilising a relationship-based approach in a contentious area of child protection. He examines how the engagement stage of the model is fundamental to determining outcomes for children and argues that a skilled approach to working will promote safeguarding practice. The case scenario, which is explored from three different perspectives, provides a useful template for social workers to reflect on their current practice. McMullin, in Chapter 4, extends our understanding of how the model can be applied to building relationships with children and young people who are 'looked after' by the state. Recognising that young people often experience a myriad of relationships with social workers throughout their care journey, she illustrates how investing in the relationship can promote wellbeing and sustain resilience. This theme is addressed in some detail in Chapter 5, when Le Chéile Mentoring and Youth Justice Support Services examine how consistent relationships have a positive impact on the educational attainment and mental health of young people. They focus on the engagement phase, highlighting the important role of the mentor in providing consistency in the relationship and encouraging us not to underestimate the power and positive influence of time-limited relationships.

In Chapter 6 Todd applies the model to relationship practice with older adults in a thought-provoking example which highlights many of the ethical and professional challenges in working with end-of-life issues. Through the powerful voice of the service user, key issues such as the right to self-determination and right to choose emerge in a context where a medical model of service delivery predominates. The reader is helped to understand how the social worker uses professional skills to protect the rights of the service user to be an expert by experience and in doing so validates the service user. This example also illustrates how professional values can be evidenced.

Clarke reinforces the concept of empowerment in Chapter 7 when he considers how the Relationship Model can be applied in the context of mental health services and significantly within a recovery ethos. Although he does not avoid examining the major challenges of stigma and biomedical approaches, his application of the model is firmly rooted in promoting person-centred care within a predominately medicalised approach. Two aspects which he opines, (1) the benefits of practitioner self-disclosure and (2) co-production and reparative relationships, support the recognition of service users as equal partners.

Interestingly, Chapter 8 examines how all the four stages of the model underpin the Northern Ireland Social Care Council (NISCC) model of building and sustaining relationships with service users and carers in the development of strategy and policy. We feel this chapter is unique in offering an understanding of how a regulator of the social care workforce has ensured that the voice of the service user is at the heart of regulatory activity. So, in addition to illustrating how this has been achieved, the voices of the service users are used to convey depth of understanding about how the process of applying the model strengthened their own sense of their power and achievement. They articulate that the personal benefits gained are multiple but the powerful message is that being acknowledged as experts brings a true sense of being heard and listened to, validating them: 'I feel valued.' Thus Chapters 6, 7 and 8 not only bring the Relationship Model to life but also offer detailed guidance about how recognition and validation are achieved through skilled intervention and professional values.

Attachment is one concept which underpins relationship-building and this is explored in different ways through Chapters 9, 10 and 12. Connor *et al.* address the components of building relationships in the context of group care settings. They highlight the importance of understanding how attachment is the foundation of key relationships and how several models of care in the United Kingdom are underpinned by this ethos. The practice example conveys important factors that contribute to relationship-building: environment, attitudes, values and verbal and nonverbal communication. Equally self-awareness and self-knowledge contribute to social workers' capacity to be receptive to the needs of others.

MacDermott and McCall address the important supervisory relationship within practice learning in Chapter 10. Again this is another unique aspect of the book, as we explore how relationship-based practice can be applied to professional learning and development. Emphasising the role of the personal narrative as well as attachment concepts, the process of transformative learning is defined using the Relationship Model. In this way the reader is helped to understand how effective learning involves a complex interplay between personal dimensions, reflective practice and a relationship which promotes trust.

McColgan's Chapter 11 integrates discussion of the diversity of terminology about working with other professionals with an explicit consideration of skills required for three of the stages of the model. Linking back to the case scenario outlined in Chapter 3, she illustrates how potential conflicts can be minimised and how empowering the service user is central to effective working even in circumstances when the power imbalance is evident, such as case conferences.

Chapter 12, by Wylie and MacDermott, draws again on a unique aspect of social work education when they consider how endings in the supervisory relationship are negotiated within professional training. They remind us that the quality of the relationship between practice educator and student can reflect the relationship between student and service user, posing challenges because of the emotional impact on all parties. Often the reluctance to acknowledge this belies the working-through of this phase. The authors set out a convincing case for encouraging the expression of these emotions through attention to endings, even though this may trigger powerful emotions of loss, anger and rejection. Ultimately, they reflect that the 'good enough' ending may suffice.

It is hoped that the book will be utilised in training and education both at undergraduate and postgraduate levels. The versatility of the book will mean that it can be used in both academic and workplace settings. It is hoped that this text could be applicable to global practice and not just within Europe.

The book will enable the reader to think critically and reflect about their practice – coupled with helpful guidance, methods and tools. This model could be used to examine service user–social worker relationships individually or as a reflective tool in supervision and to assist greater awareness. The model might enable us to critically reflect on the development of relationships in four stages. It does not aim to be prescriptive but gives some explanation as to how relationships might develop, and this can be changeable as people can find themselves in different parts of the model at any given time.

1. The first stage is engaging – the start of the relationship-building process – and this can be done by using 'soft skills', sharing ideas and thoughts and building a rapport.

2. Stage two is about negotiating and agreeing expectations, limits and boundaries to the relationship and contracting.

3. Stage three is about enabling change and giving information, choice and advice. Key aspects include building confidence and self-esteem, encouraging and motivating.

4. Stage four introduces endings, and values the ending as much as the initial beginnings of the relationship-building process.

The chapters are designed to cover a wide range of settings and service user groups as relationships are fundamental to social work practice, youth and community work and other health professionals. As the contributors to the book also reflect diversity in professional contexts and settings, the reader is encouraged to re-imagine how the Relationship-Based Model could be applied.

References

Hood, R., Goldacre, A., Grant, R. and Jones, R. (2016) 'Exploring demand and provision in English child protection services.' *British Journal of Social Work 46*, 4, 923–942.

Ward, L. and Barnes, M. (2016) 'Transforming practice with older people through an ethic of care.' *British Journal of Social Work 46*, 4, 906–923.

Chapter 1

BUILDING RELATIONSHIPS IN SOCIAL WORK

A 4 Stage Relationship Model

Cheryl McMullin

It is hoped that reading this chapter will both enable you, the reader, to think about your own experience and be a guide to helping you understand the steps involved in relationship-based practice. As an experienced practitioner/educator I observed that relationships were becoming less important compared to interventions, assessing or being able to access services. I found this challenging and frustrating as time to build relationships could not be prioritised due to other demands, for example, paperwork and recording. I would argue that there is not enough value given to building relationships. I would consider relationship-building to be an intervention in itself and the foundation of good practice.

Reflection on my own practice experience over the last fifteen years has allowed me to develop a 4 Stage Relationship Model that encourages us to be more aware of the stages of the relationship building process, and to Engage, Negotiate, Enable and consider Endings. This model, which is introduced in this chapter, is a simple but useful way to evaluate self-knowledge of the relationship-building process and, as the other chapters in this book illustrate, can be applied to understand and assess relationships that were developed using other methods or models, in a variety of social work contexts. This model is not exclusive to practitioners but can be used in partnership with service users, sharing the knowledge and enabling change for themselves; this will be explored in more detail by service users in Chapter 8 of this book.

This chapter will address some of the themes and definitions that have emerged in the current literature on relational and relationship-based practice (Cooper 2014; Hennessey 2011; Megele 2015; Ruch, Turney and Ward 2010; Trevithick 2003; Winter 2011). Consideration has been given to some important issues that impact on the development of relationships in social work practice, for example the variety of relationships, anti-oppressive practice, resilience, resistance, communication styles, social work role including 'use of self', emotional intelligence and reflective practice. These themes give some context to why and how the 4 Stage Relationship Model might be applied and useful in practice.

Relationship-based practice

Relationships are central to the work that practitioners carry out, as nothing else will be effective if the basic relationship-building process is not achieved. Collins and Collins (1981) and Trevithick (2012) highlight that the client–worker relationship should be 'at the heart of social work' (Trevithick 2012, p.13). It can be argued that this continues to be a very relevant and poignant definition that needs to be revisited in current practice. However, students and practitioners are finding it increasingly difficult to integrate this concept into practice because of all the other competing demands and components of the role. Cooper (2014) discusses relationship-based practice in 'turbulent times' but highlights the necessity of this in social work practice. It is hoped that the 4 Stage Model may enable students and practitioners to focus on the importance of relationships and how to work with the opportunities and challenges.

Relationship-based practice has been aligned with Carl Rogers' (1967) person-centred approach because it promotes an equitable relationship between service user and practitioner. The service user is the expert; however, this can be conflicted and challenging, especially for example when having to make child protection referrals in either the statutory or voluntary sector. Practitioners have to intervene or challenge service users in their decisions if there is assessed harm to themselves and/or others. This can bring about mistrust and anger from service users; however, the model highlights that if you have established a good working relationship you can work together even if there is disagreement.

Murphy, Duggan and Joseph (2012) have concerns with the person-centred approach that underpins some relational-based practice, suggesting that this approach in contemporary social work practice is not compatible. Lindsay (2013) highlights the strengths and limitations of the person-centred approach in social work practice and concurs with Murphy *et al.* (2012) that in statutory social work or dealing with risk the social worker has to intervene. In my experience it is how you deliver difficult messages and decisions that can make the difference, for example, demonstrating empathy and compassion. This will be explored in more detail throughout the following chapters of the book with the application of the 4 Stage Relationship Model integrated into practice experience and knowledge.

The psychodynamic approach includes the theory from a psychological perspective explaining human behaviour in terms of our motivations, urges and drives (Lindsay 2013). The psychosocial approach blends theory from the psychodynamic approach considering both internal factors like thoughts and feelings and external factors such as socio-economic and political issues that impact on behaviour and relationships. It can be argued that psychosocial approaches can offer much learning and application in social work practice. However, neither the psychodynamic nor psychosocial approaches are mutually exclusive, and they highlight the complexity of defining relationship-based social work (Ruch *et al.* 2010, cited in Megele 2015).

The importance of relationships

Relationships in social work are crucial because they are the foundation of the work we do with service users, professionals, colleagues, experts and other service providers. Working with others and building relationships is often what interests people in a career in social work. Hennessey (2011) highlights that it is the relational dimension of social work that attracts social work students to fulfil the need to 'work with people'. There are huge benefits from relationships in terms of building networks, learning and development. Social work practice needs to be less mechanistic, managerial and procedural; from my own practice experience a mantra used to be 'If it wasn't written down it didn't happen', meaning that recording, reports and assessing were prioritised.

Relationship-building needs to be re-established in current practice given the criticisms of social work practice and feedback from service users highlighted in this chapter. It is hoped that the Relationship Model will allow practitioners to refocus on what is more important in practice rather than prioritising bureaucratic processes, that permission is given to practitioners to use this as a model of intervention and that the work involved in relationship-building is validated.

Communication

Thompson (2011) and Good (2001) illustrated that communication with one another is how relationships, communities and societies are made and maintains that communication in the traditional 'caring professions' is a basic building block and arguably crucial to good practice. If communication fails it can have serious consequences, highlighted in outcomes and recommendations from Serious Case Reviews (Laming 2003; Munro 2011). It is hard to believe in this modern age that there are still so many problems with communication given the various methods available in relation to email, telephone, text and Skype. Perhaps it highlights that it is still the face to face or direct communication skills that are the most essential and effective in practice. Communication and developing this skill is essential for the application of the Relationship Model.

Practitioners when building relationships need to consider other variables that may impede their ability to communicate effectively, for example, language barriers, gender or cultural differences, disability and working with different age groups. To overcome these challenges we need to develop our knowledge of different service users' circumstances and adapt to and learn new skills for each individual, as well as not to oversimplify the challenges. The conflict for practitioners can be between wanting to spend time 'getting to know' service users and the pressure of 'getting the work done'. It is important that we can be creative when overcoming barriers, for example using service users' interests such as art, music, drama, technology or sport as a means of communication. The first stage in the 4 Stage Model is engagement, and preparation for contact and communication skills are so important to initiate the process. Practitioners need to be mindful of what will enable or impede the communication and engagement in the initial relationship-building phase.

The list is not exhaustive but we need to think differently about how we communicate and build relationships with service users. The environment, time and day of the week can impact on how the relationship might evolve; for example, a lot of social work occurs in offices or homes on a 9-to-5 basis. Practitioners will often say that some of the best opportunities for communication will have happened when driving with a service user in the car, in a non-threatening environment. There are many variables that might impact on our interaction and communication, and we need to be mindful of how these other factors might inhibit or enable relationship-building, for example, even the time of year, especially Christmas, which can be particularly emotive.

The 4 Stage Relationship Model

There is no 'perfect way' to build relationships and we are all unique and have different personalities and strengths that can enable and inhibit our ability to nurture positive relationships. The 4 Stage Relationship Model shown in the figure overleaf is not meant to be prescriptive in relation to how we do this but tries to go some way in breaking the process down. It could be used to examine service user–practitioner relationships individually or as a reflective tool in supervision and to assist greater awareness.

The model might enable us to critically reflect on the development of relationships in four stages: Engage, Negotiate, Enable and Endings. It gives us an understanding of the momentum within relationships, as people can find themselves in different stages of the model at any given time; for example, the shift from prevention to protection can impact on the relationship between the practitioner and the service user. The model is cyclical and can be repeated; for instance, you may complete work in the Endings stage with a service user only to find in a couple of months you receive a new referral allocation for them and return to the beginning (Engage stage). The service user and practitioner might be at different stages of the relationship, for example, one party being 'stuck' at one stage, the other perceiving the relationship to be at a different stage. In all relationships there will be occasions when people are resistant to change, and it is acknowledged how incredibly difficult change can be.

The idea is that we can move backwards and forwards through different stages depending on what may be occurring in the relationship. It is possible to go from Engage straight to Endings and never have the opportunity to go through the Negotiate and Enable stages. A practitioner and service user relationship might also be sustained over many years and, in my experience, you could go through the process many times over depending on what circumstance or changes occur in the service user's life.

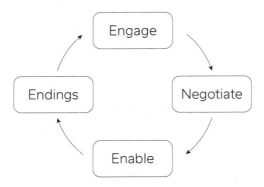

Engage (Stage 1) is the start of the relationship-building process and engagement; this can be done by using 'soft skills', sharing ideas and thoughts and building a rapport.

Negotiate (Stage 2) is about negotiating and agreeing expectations, limits and boundaries to the relationship and contracting, for example, addressing consent and confidentiality. This involves skills such as explaining what you will be doing, how you will work with the service user and why you are involved in their lives.

Enable (Stage 3) is about the process of enabling change and giving information choice and advice. There needs to be open communication – to be realistic, positive and reflect on progress. Discuss interventions and resources, inhibitors and enabling factors. This stage is about building confidence and self-esteem, encouraging and motivating.

Endings (Stage 4) involves introducing endings and valuing the ending process as much as the start of the relationship-building process. There needs to be reflection and evaluation on what has worked well, strengths for the future and coping strategies, signposting to other services for further support.

Engaging

When initiating the relationship-building process we need to be clear about each other's expectations, role and limitations. The practitioner needs to use active listening skills, values of honesty, openness, clear communication, to share ideas and give choice. Choice is very powerful and an important element in empowering a service user, for example, what services or resources they receive. This should help to enable the relationship; however, we have to be mindful of potential existing barriers to the social work practitioner relationship, which are misunderstanding, confusion, anger, resentment, fear, resistance and apathy. Engaging could take a number of tries and it can be a lengthy process for some service users to build trust. The importance of this stage is that you can build from the initial engagement through all stages of the relationship-building process.

Negotiating

Negotiation is the process of agreement, partnership and, as much as possible, shared understanding of the key issues and problems. Empowerment and respect need to be evident in the relationship at this stage when there may be differences in opinions and potential solutions. The inhibitors to this might be different expectations, both parties struggling with agreed assessment or planning. In this stage the relationship may be on a superficial level and there is potential for minimising issues; mistrust may even be evident in the relationship. However, even if there are challenges and difficult decisions that need to be made it's important to build on what has occurred and consider what has worked well previously.

Enabling

Enabling involves appreciating the benefits of the relationship and the intervention, choices and resources. This is a mutually advantageous partnership with motivation, confidence and self-esteem increased. The inhibitor to this stage may be that trying to change at this time is too difficult. The service user may enjoy the professional contact but is unable to move forwards or action decisions/plans. This may result in a service user feeling they should disengage from the relationship and social work intervention. At this stage it is important perhaps to prioritise or to take small steps and consider any other resources that might be needed to achieve positive change.

Endings

It is important at the initial enabling stage to discuss potential endings and integrate this with expectations of the relationship. Where possible endings should be planned with agreement as to how this might happen, for example reduced contact or phased approach. Another crisis may occur for the service user and impact on the ending process and the relationship goes back to another stage in the process. If a service user has had poor experiences of relationships ending they may feel rejected and sometimes the 'saying goodbye' can be too difficult and endings can be sabotaged. Consideration needs to be given to dependency on the relationship and enjoying the professional contact. It is hoped that independence and a mutually positive experience has been achieved. Good endings require preparation and often a ritual, for example, a final informal session, a cup of tea/coffee, a meal or a professional handover to another service.

Social work role

The social work practitioner occupies a rapidly changing landscape. The profession has to balance and respond to social developments in the wake of increased regulation and auditing demands, cuts to frontline services alongside increased expectations that practitioners can build relationships with service users which are enabling and empowering. Parker and Doel (2013) highlight that the development of the social work profession has nearly been at the cost of compassion and the service user relationship itself. These competing demands can be currently summarised that there are greater need and higher standards with fewer resources. Social workers would welcome more resources and greater government support for the work highlighted in research by Unison and Community Care (2014). Notwithstanding all the difficulties and challenges it is possible to build positive relationships but it's important that we are aware of the complexities. Thompson (2009) highlights the importance of being realistic and for practitioners to be aware of the personal and professional challenges when working with people. The model can be used as a tool to aid critical reflection and address some of the challenges and to reinforce the view that relationship-building is still a key skill for practitioners.

Reflective practice

Critical reflection is the cornerstone of social work practice and has become integral to good supervision, enabling practitioners to reflect on the challenges of working in contemporary social work practice. Healey (2012) describes the importance of critical reflection in the caring professions and how it can build a sense of professional purpose. Critical reflection gives practitioners the opportunity to reflect on practice issues and develop their knowledge, skills and values. Applying the Relationship Model to perhaps difficult or complex cases in supervision may enable us to understand how we might overcome challenges or adapt our approach. Thompson (2009) highlights the need to be open to new ideas and other perspectives even if they challenge our own. If there are blocks to supervision, for example the line manager and practitioner have different pressures, agenda or opinions, this can inhibit the supervision process.

Supervision is important, so we need to think how to create opportunities for good supervision, for example, the ability to choose or change supervisor or have different types of supervision, such as, group or clinical supervision. Turbett (2014) highlights that social workers who take pride in their work will value and seize further training and other opportunities for personal development. If a practitioner is able to have a good reflective supervisory relationship this should then be mirrored through their practice and relationships with service users.

Resilience, resistance and aggression

Relationships require time, patience and negotiation and they also require personal strength and resilience. When working with service users the work can be both short term and long term, for example you could potentially work with people for a number of years.

This requires skills in maintaining relationships over a long period of time. In short-term work you could be required to intervene quickly or in a crisis situation, which requires engaging quickly with service users when they are most vulnerable.

In social work, practitioners are likely at some time in their careers to experience resistance or aggression from service users. Broadly speaking in social work there are two strands of service users, those who request help from caring professionals owing to an issue or problem they are experiencing and those whom professionals engage with owing to the potential risk of harm that service users pose to themselves and/or others. This is inherent in the nature of working directly with people and offering a service to the public, as in many other professions. This may be because of poor previous experiences of social work or professionals and worries about potential punitive interventions. This will then have an impact on any relationship established with a service user as this can occur out of frustration, loss of control and disempowerment. Taylor (2011) advises that relationships can become strained due to misunderstanding or unrealistic expectations; however, it is important to make the distinction between decisions being professional rather than personal.

Furthermore, if we are negotiating or challenging difficult situations or making decisions services users do not agree with we need to consider the way in which those messages and decisions are delivered. If you have very frequent contact and good relationships with service users sometimes they may find it difficult to distinguish between the personal and professional and this is a delicate balance to be negotiated and established at the first (engaging) stage of the Relationship Model and relationship-building process. Practitioners need to make better use of colleagues and supervision for support when experiencing aggression and resistance so that they have the opportunity to reflect on their own strengths, self-worth, values, generosity and kindness, despite others' negative behaviour (Taylor 2011). If you are committed to building relationships and working with people there needs to be some level of appreciation that relationships are dynamic, especially when working in complex situations.

Professional relationships

When working as a practitioner there are numerous types of professional relationships, for example with other social workers, key workers, administrators, youth and community workers, health professionals, justice and legal professionals, interpreters, educators/academics and experts. Social work practitioners often have to adapt and engage with people with varying degrees of understanding and knowledge about each other's area of expertise. Social work's own identity needs to be re-established in the caring professions as it is often perceived as being punitive and has a negative public and professional image. Croisdale-Appleby (2014) highlighted the complexity of the role well when suggesting a social worker was practitioner, professional and social scientist.

Consideration needs to be given to multiagency working and improving relationships. Despite the complexities and challenges, good relationships need to be maintained with all the key stakeholders within the public sector, voluntary sector and local communities. This will be explored in more detail in Chapter 11 in relation to developing professional relationships and the application of the model.

Service user and practitioner boundaries

When considering professional boundaries with service users, cognisance needs to be taken of the purpose of the relationship, regardless of if it is voluntary or involuntary. O'Leary, Ming-Sum and Ruch (2013) suggest that there are essential criteria for the relationship, a purpose and a function for that relationship to develop. When setting boundaries we have to consider that this is subjective and based on previous experiences and learning. When applying the model we should consider that every circumstance and individual is unique. Practitioners have to adapt and develop their relationship-building skills in each circumstance and stage of the model when negotiating boundaries with service users.

Service users and carers

Service users and carers' perspectives on the services they receive should be considered fundamental to service delivery. Healey (2012) discusses the service user perspective of social work services and emphasises that they want practitioners to 'engage with them in an open, authentic and warm manner' (p.8). However, she also highlights some of the challenges like choice in service provision, ability to express themselves, diversity of service user views on their own circumstances and the compulsory nature of service provision. If service users do not have choice or control this can impact on the relationship-building process and develop mistrust or disempowerment.

When reflecting on social work practice as a service and comparing it to other service providers it can fall short as service users get little (or more often, no) choice in their practitioner. Often if a service user asks to change social worker this request can be perceived as resistance or reluctance to engage. Perhaps within teams and organisations more thought needs to go into matching service users and workers together or offering choice. Care-experienced young people may often experience multiple practitioners from different teams and this can impact on trust, self-esteem, feelings of rejection, attachments, positive role modelling and service provision/care planning. McFadden *et al.*'s (2012) research in resilience in social work highlights that continuity in the relationship becomes compromised owing to excessive caseloads and high staff turnover.

It is important that practitioners never lose sight of the impact they may have on service users, and this relates back to anti-oppressive practice issues and power. Often practitioners may experience hostility from service users but we need to remember that this is sometimes the only way people can express themselves, especially when they feel vulnerable or threatened. Consideration needs to be given to the unique life histories and narratives of service users highlighted in *The National Occupational Standards for Social Work* (2011), and practitioners need to be mindful of this when building relationships. Practitioners can become a significant adult in the lives of the most vulnerable and we should not minimise our intervention or impact. Practitioners should appreciate the value of their work. Doel *et al.*'s (2010) research suggests that there is not enough known about good practice as compliments are not recorded but complaints are.

Ruch *et al.* (2010) reflect that, 'At its best, what social work can offer people in need of help is a supportive and understanding relationship which will enable them to resolve their difficulties and feel enhanced other than undermined in the process' (p.7). Research by Beresford, Croft and Ashead (2008) highlighted beneficial experiences in the relationship between service users and practitioner so that it was like a 'friendship' and these were often seen as valuable and unique. Further research carried out by Perlinski, Blom and Morén (2012) featured the importance of trust in the practitioner–service user relationship; these outcomes would concur with research from Mitchell (2012) that social work practitioners should not underestimate the value of 'being there' and being interested and responsive when working with people.

Power and anti-oppressive practice

Practitioners are perceived as having significant power, influence and access to services, expertise and resources. Parker and Doel (2013) highlight that good professionals are aware of the advantages and disadvantages 'that professional status brings' (p.31). There is a conflict within perceived power and the actual ability to help and enable others successfully, for example, when resources are scarce and practitioners can request services that might not be attained. This can impact on the relationship-building process as service users may really need a resource to enable positive changes and this can lead to dissatisfaction with the service and in turn the relationship.

In practice, at worst, service users may fear that 'social workers will snatch my children away' and at best the professionals are perceived as supportive and able to access valuable resources, for example, a referral for counselling. Given the negative media coverage and limitations on resources this means practitioners find it increasingly difficult to do the 'good stuff', for example, therapeutic work. Practitioners intervene when people are at their most vulnerable, therefore there will always be an initial power differential but what is important is how we address this. Practitioners can lose appreciation of their perceived power alongside fears, hopes and expectations service users may have of the relationship. In an increasing climate of 'defensive practice' it is all too often that practitioners lose sight of the power dynamic owing to experiencing frustration or powerlessness in their own professional role.

In order to overcome some of these potential barriers we need always to be aware of power and to be honest, transparent and share the challenges. Practitioners when applying the model need to be creative and try to use themselves more as a resource and develop the relationship, for example, having and making opportunities for 'trouble-free talk' and activities. Butler, Ford and Tregaskis (2007) would concur that social workers' strengths should not just be limited to their professional skills.

Emotional intelligence

Emotional intelligence is an important skill to develop when building relationships. Grant, Kinman and Alexander (2014) emphasise that emotional intelligence is the ability to perceive emotions and their relevance in social work practice. Cognisance should be given to the use of emotional intelligence and de-constructing a situation to consider how others may be thinking and feeling. Grant *et al.* (2014) discuss that emotional intelligence has many positive outcomes and can be achieved in, for example, negotiating, confidence-building, decision-making and trust. These mirror important aspects of relational social work practice and the emphasis is on practitioners becoming skilled at this in practice. This is relevant to relationship-based practice as perception, self-awareness and empathy are important when building relationships.

Use of self

Megele (2015) suggests that 'good relationship-based practice requires effective use of self'; this highlights that practitioners need to be encouraged to develop their own professional style. The Relationship Model addresses some of the components that are needed to enable a positive relationship; for example, a practitioner may need to blend the professional skills of respect, empathy and equality with other qualities and interests they have that can be incorporated into practice. The 'use of self' is what shapes our practice. Thompson (2009) discusses personal effectiveness and that it underpins the other skills involved when working with people. Hennessey (2011) discusses how as social workers we can use ourselves creatively; a student practitioner highlighted that 'part of yourself is part of the practice' (p.5) and that, although we are professional, our personality and our own culture and values are not mutually exclusive and they will impact on our ability to engage and form relationships. It can be argued that personality, warmth and fun are traits that can enable relationship-building. Baines (2007), cited in Turbett (2014), highlights that humour, courtesy and associated people skills can achieve much in even difficult and challenging circumstances. Practitioners need to become comfortable at developing their own style rather than a superficial approach. To this end, 'use of self' and 'self-knowledge' must be integral elements within initial training for developing practitioners' ability to view themselves as a resource.

There needs to be a revival in showing kindness and caring in practice and giving people hope for their future. Compassion can be demonstrated in small acts like giving someone a lift home, accompanying them to an appointment or a telephone call. Practitioners need to be caring and reliable: these are crucial factors when building trust and respect in relationships.

Reflection points

- Consider 'tuning in' to your own feelings when preparing for contact. Consider how you will introduce yourself. Be confident, prepared and explain what organisation you represent (and have identification). Use your observation and self-awareness skills to consider body language and nonverbal cues. Smile and be positive if it is appropriate and 'tune in' to the service user's expressions and body language towards you.

- Consider how you explain confidentiality and consent issues: make it simple and, although this is procedural, reassure service users. Think about ice-breaker questions and some 'trouble-free talk' checking in on how people are: 'How are things with you at the moment?' or 'How are you getting on?' Consider what the purpose of the session is. What might be discussed at the session? If you don't address everything or need to respond to something else going on for the service user then go back again another time.

- Use a variety of questioning styles like open, closed, reflective, clarifying and scaling questions. Sometimes it is appropriate to use the best hope question, for example, 'If it could be different or in an ideal world what would you like to happen?', or solution-focused questions, 'How do you think things could be improved?'

- When ending a session summarise and reflect on what was discussed and consider making plans for the next meeting and give contact details. What is the outcome of the meeting? What has been agreed and expected for the next session? Be realistic and don't make promises you can't keep or give information if you are unsure. It is always respectful to thank service users for meeting with you and allowing you into their lives.

It is important to recognise that to over-analyse relationships can be counterproductive. Relationships should evolve naturally and are unique to the context and circumstances in which they exist. The Relationship Model is a tool that can enable students and practitioners to try and understand how and why relationships evolve and what might be occurring. It is hoped that students and practitioners can use the model effectively within their practice to help enable meaningful relationship-building in the definitive stages of engaging, negotiating, enabling and endings. The other chapters in this book will apply the model in different settings and utilise one or various parts of it to illustrate its effectiveness when applied to practice.

References

Baines, D. (ed.) (2007) *Doing Anti-Oppressive Practice: Building Transformative Politicized Social Work*. Nova Scotia: Fernwood.

Beresford, P., Croft, S. and Ashead, L. (2008) 'We don't see her as a practitioner: a service user case study of the importance of practioner's relationship and humanity.' *British Journal of Social Work 38*, 1388–1470.

Butler, A., Ford, D. and Tregaskis, C. (2007) 'Who do we think we are? Self and reflexivity in social work practice.' *Qualitative Social Work 6*, 281.

Collins, J. and Collins, M. (1981) *Achieving Change in Social Work*. London: Heinemann.

Cooper, A. (2014) *Making Space: Relationship-Based Practice in Turbulent Times*. Maldon: Centre for Social Work Practice. Available at http://cfswp.org/education/paper. php?s=making-space-relationship-based-practice-in-turbulent-times, accessed on 2 November 2016.

Croisdale-Appleby, D. (2014) *Re-Visioning Social Work Education: An Independent Review*. London: Department of Health.

Doel, M., Allmark, P., Conway, P., Cowburn, M. *et al.* (2010) 'Professional boundaries: crossing the line or in the shadows.' *British Journal of Social Work 40*, 6, 1866–1889.

Good, D. (2001) 'Language and Communication.' In C. Fraser, B. Burchell, D. Hay, and G. Dunveen (eds) *Introducing Social Psychology*. Cambridge: Polity.

Grant, L., Kinman, G. and Alexander, K. (2014) 'What's all this talk about emotion? Developing emotional intelligence in social work students.' *Social Work Education 33*, 7, 874–889.

Healey, K. (2012) *Social Work Methods and Skills*. Basingstoke: Palgrave Macmillan.

Hennessey, R. (2011) *Relationship Skills in Social Work*. London: Sage.

Laming, H. (2003) *The Victoria Climbié Inquiry Report*. London: HMSO.

Lindsay, T. (2013) *Social Work Intervention* (2nd edn). London: Sage.

McFadden, P., Taylor, B.J., Campbell, A. and McQuilkin, J. (2012) 'Systematically identifying relevant research: case study on child protection social workers' resilience.' *Research on Social Work Practice 22*, 6, 626–636.

Megele, C. (2015) *Psychodynamic and Relationship-Based Practice*. Northwich: Critical Publishing.

Mitchell, F. (2012) *Using the Social Work Relationship to Promote Recovery for Adolescents Who Have Experienced Abuse and Neglect*. Stirling: School of Applied Social Science. Available at withscotland.org/download/using-the-social-work-model-to-promote-recovery-for-adolescents-who-have-experienced-abuse-and-neglect.pdf, accessed on 13 December, 2016.

Munro, E. (2011) *The Munro Review of Child Protection: Final Report: A Child-Centred System*. London: Stationery Office.

Murphy, D., Duggan, M. and Joseph, S. (2012) 'Relationship-based social work and its compatibility with person-centred approach: principled versus instrumental perspectives.' *British Journal of Social Work 43*, 4, 703–719.

O'Leary, P., Ming-Sum, T. and Ruch, G. (2013) 'The boundaries of the social work relationship revisited: towards a connected, inclusive and dynamic conceptualisation.' *British Journal of Social Work 43* ,1, 135–153.

Parker, J. and Doel, M. (2013) *Professional Social Work*. London: Sage.

Pernlinski, M., Blom, B. and Morén, S. (2012) 'Getting a sense of the client: working methods in the personal social services in Sweden.' *Journal of Social Work 13*, 5, 508–532.

Rogers, C. R. (1967) *A Therapist's View of Psychotherapy: 'On Becoming a Person'*. London: Constable.

Ruch, G., Turney, D. and Ward, A. (2010) *Relationship-Based Social Work: 'Getting to the Heart of Practice'*. London: Jessica Kingsley Publishers.

Taylor, B. J. (2011) *Working with Aggression and Resistance in Social Work*. Exeter: Learning Matters.

Thompson, N. (2009) *People Skills* (3rd edn). Basingstoke: Palgrave Macmillan.

Thompson, N. (2011) *Effective Communication* (2nd edn). Basingstoke: Palgrave Macmillan.

Trevithick, P. (2003) 'Effective relationship-based practice: a theoretical exploration.' *Journal of Social Work Practice 17*, 2, 163–176.

Trevithick, P. (2012) *Social Work Skills and Knowledge* (3rd edn). Buckingham: Open University Press/McGraw-Hill.

Turbett, C. (2014) *Doing Radical Social Work*. Basingstoke: Palgrave Macmillan.

UK Commission for Employment and Skills. (2011) *National Occupational Standards for Social Work*. London: UKCES. Available at www.ccwales.org.uk/qualifications-and-nos-finder/n/social-work/, accessed on 2 November 2016.

Unison and Community Care (2014) *Social Work Watch – Inside an Average Day in Social Work*. Available at https://www.unison.org.uk/content/uploads/2014/06/TowebSocial-Work-Watch-final-report-PDF2.pdf, accessed on 2 November 2016.

Winter, K. (2011) *Building Relationships and Communicating with Young Children: A Practical Guide for Social Workers*. Oxford: Routledge.

Chapter 2

RELATIONSHIP-BASED PRACTICE: CHALLENGES AND OPPORTUNITIES IN CONTEMPORARY SOCIAL WORK

John McLaughlin

Over the past three decades the welfare state in the UK has undergone profound organisational and professional change due to the effects of neoliberalism and new public management (NPM). The social, political, economic and ideological effects of these global doctrines on social welfare organisations in the 1980s and 1990s radically transformed not only the organisational context in which social work is practised but also the nature and function of social work with all service user groups within the UK (Lorenz 2005). A major consequence of these changes at practice level in adult services, for example, resulted in a move away from direct face to face therapeutic work with service users to a preoccupation with assessment of need and risk and the rationing of resources and services (Lymbery and Postle 2015; Webb 2006). In essence, the relational aspects of a holistic and psychosocial focus on practice with users, families and carers became increasingly subordinated to the needs and priorities of managers and their organisation across all service user groups (Rogowski 2010).

The impact of neoliberalism and managerialism on social work in the UK

The rise of new public management as an ideology and policy initiative in the UK in the 1980s had a profound impact on the organisation and management of public sector organisations. The new public management, also known as 'managerialism', first came to prominence in the UK under the New Right Conservative government in the 1980s and was responsible for promoting and transporting business techniques and practice from the private to the public sector with the aim of enhancing the quality and efficiency of public services (Klikauer 2015; Pollitt and Bouckaert 2011). The common core of this neoliberalist doctrine, characterised by marketisation, managerialism, privatisation and an emphasis on output measurement and performance targets (McDonald 2006), radically reshaped community care policy and practice throughout the UK. The 1988 Griffiths Report and the subsequent 1990 NHS and Community Care Act ('People First', DHSS (NI) 1990), which introduced the purchaser–provider split, laid the basis for a market-based approach in the delivery of community care and led to the transformation of social work into a business (Harris 2003). In their analysis of managerialism and its impact on public sector organisations and service delivery processes, Tsui and Cheung (2004, pp.438–440) summarise the concept's key characteristics:

- the client is a customer (not service consumer)

- the manager (not the frontline staff) as the key

- the staff are employees (not professionals)

- management knowledge (not common sense or professional knowledge) as the dominant model of knowledge

- the market (not society or the community) as the environment

- efficiency (not effectiveness) as the yardstick

- cash and contracts (not care and concern) as the foundation of relationships

- quality is equated with standardisation and documentation.

It is important to acknowledge, however, that managerialism is not just a series of managerial and service delivery innovations but is rather an administrative and organisational system as well as a set of ideas about the role of the state in society and public management (Van de Walle and Hammerschmid 2011). As Tsui and Cheung (2004) suggest, a significant focus of managerialism is on markets, managers and measurement with the goal of achieving efficiency, effectiveness and value for money within the organisation. In the UK context, under the community care arrangements and the purchaser–provider split, the social work role was radically re-defined whereby social workers became commissioners of services instead of direct providers of services within a mixed economy of welfare (Lymbery and Postle 2015). Within this technology of care known as care management, social work became increasingly understood as a technical and functional activity whose central role was the assessment of need and risk and the co-ordination of care for service users rather than relationship-building and providing direct therapeutic support to service users and carers (Dustin 2006; Lymbery 2005).

Within an organisational context of neoliberal managed care and the increasing proceduralisation, regulation and routinisation of practice, social work has become, it has been argued, de-skilled and de-professionalised due to the increasing erosion of opportunities for practitioners to apply their full repertoire of professional knowledge, skills and values in practice (Carey 2003; Dustin 2012; Ray, Bernard and Phillips 2009). Research by Weinberg et al. (2003), for example, who surveyed 60 care managers in seven community-based social service teams in England, found that while care managers spent a significant proportion of their time in the office on routine paperwork and 27 per cent of their time undertaking assessments, only 5 per cent of their time was spent providing counselling and support to service users and carers. What is clear in the literature is that since the 1990s not only has the social work role in community care become increasingly process-driven, reductionist and administratively focused to meet government targets and limit public expenditure, but also the nature of the relationship between the service user and social worker has shifted from one of support to a contractual, time-limited and task-oriented encounter (Bogues 2008; Ruch, Turney and Ward 2010; Tsui and Cheung 2004).

The increasing bureaucratisation and managerialisation of social work within all fields of practice throughout the UK reflects the continued dominance of neoliberalism and its negative impact on the capacity of frontline practitioners to provide help and support to vulnerable service users, children and families (Rogowski 2013). Webb (2006, p.121) succinctly captures this managerialist shift to highlight the demise of relational practice in statutory social services work: 'In social work we can observe this in the tendency towards ephemeral but intense relations between practitioners and clients whereby fast, over-loaded and time-pressured contacts become the norm.' As highlighted by Trevithick (2014), within a 'compliance culture' of targets, procedures and performance indicators, meeting a target doesn't mean meeting a need, as problems carry an emotional dimension. The challenge for practitioners within a radically changed and highly managerialised health and social care organisational culture in the UK is to find creative ways to address both the needs of the organisation as well as effectively responding to the practical and emotional needs of service users and carers.

The following section explores the impact of neoliberal policy developments in adult services and social work with children and families and the challenges and opportunities in promoting relationship-based approaches in social work practice. This is also echoed in other chapters throughout the book, particularly in Chapters 3–6, 9 and 11.

Adult services

Although the growth and influence of managerialism and the marketisation of services has been experienced in all fields of health and social care services in the UK over the past decades, this has been especially pervasive within the area of community care. Social work with older people is one area of practice where the marketisation of welfare and the colonisation of professional practice by bureaucratised and managerialist practices has been particularly evident (Lymbery and Postle 2015; Ray et al. 2009). While historically social work practice with older people has generally been seen as simply involving the provision of services or practical help rather than acknowledging the emotional needs they may also have (Payne 2012), neoliberal policy developments in community care since the 1980s further reinforced the stereotypical view that older people do not require professional social work services that could respond to the complexity of their needs in a more holistic way. Under this ageist construction of the 'dependent' individual who needed only 'care' (Ray 2014; Thompson and Thompson 2001), social care assessment and practice came to be viewed as a technical task that could be managed through administrative-oriented practice and care brokerage within the care management process (Lymbery 2005). According to McDonald, Postle and Dawson (2007, cited in Ray et al. 2009, p.153), 'Community care practice has become an exercise in resource finding within a market economy', characterised by standardised assessments and a focus on the task of determining eligibility for services. Such a reductive and narrow 'administrative' view of the needs of older people neglects the structural disadvantage, life course inequalities and ageism they can experience and the contribution social work can make to challenging these aspects of oppression in later life (Richards 2000). It has been argued that routinised practice dominated by administrative procedures reduces the opportunities for practitioners to work directly and in a more holistic way with individuals to address the diversity of complex practice situations (Ray 2014).

However, in gerontological social work, the 'co-production' of the assessment of older people's complex needs requires high levels of practice ability and expertise that employs biographical and strengths-based approaches to reach an understanding of an individual in their social context (Richards 2000). Within a relationship of trust, the use of a narrative approach to assessment with older people is important as it not only conveys respect for the service user as a person but also provides a person-centred and holistic assessment that acknowledges and addresses other possible issues or concerns that may be affecting their quality of life and emotional wellbeing. According to Tanner and Harris:

> If older people are not given the space to tell their stories, or if these are only heard through the limited ears of narrow, managerially defined criteria that ignore broader social, psychological and emotional dimensions of experience, issues that are crucial to the older person's wellbeing will be overlooked or ignored. (2008, p.141)

As a specialist area of work with older people, gerontological social work is concerned with maintaining and enhancing the quality of life and wellbeing of older people and their families and with promoting independence, autonomy and dignity (Milne *et al.* 2014), and social workers are arguably well placed to respond to the complexity and multiple needs that older people may experience at times of loss, change and transition. In addition, because of their professional knowledge and skills, social workers can make a valuable contribution to supporting older people living with long-term conditions and their carers, who themselves may benefit from support and advocacy from skilled practitioners at times of crisis. As suggested in Chapter 1, the

4 Stage Relationship Model highlights the centrality of the sensitive use of self in the process of engaging, negotiation, enabling change and managing and facilitating endings within the social work process. In situations where older people may have high support needs due to dementia or end-of-life care, for example, or where safeguarding issues are being assessed, service users and carers require a skilled response from practitioners who take the time to form meaningful relationships, are sympathetic and who are prepared to listen. Building a relationship with the older person and their carer through the skilled 'use of self' (Dewane 2006) can facilitate effective psychosocial assessment of needs, particularly in situations of risk, uncertainty and transition. Research in Northern Ireland (Boyle 2015), which examined the roles and tasks of gerontological social workers, found that time for direct social work with older people and carers was being significantly eroded due to high caseloads, crippling levels of bureaucracy and a preoccupation with targets. However, despite the effects of managerialism on the social work role, staff highlighted the importance of relationship-building for effective practice with service user and carers. The study also reported that, in addition to their routine co-ordination and administration roles, social workers also provided time and emotional support to users and carers through counselling and advocacy as well as offering other forms of therapeutic support to build capacity and resilience to help them cope at times of crisis and transition (Ward, Barnes and Gahan 2012). As an ethically driven practice, gerontological social work affords practitioners the opportunity not only to provide a person-centred and relationship-based service to older people and their carers but also to develop practice with a clear focus on advocacy, social justice and human rights. According to Hil (2014), 'The most important part of social work is not in pursuing measureable outputs, but in developing meaningful and empowering human relationships.'

Personalisation

The trend towards personalisation and personalised care introduced by the New Labour government in *Putting People First* (Department of Health 2007) represents a policy framework whose aim is to introduce a 'new vision' in the 'transformation' and modernisation of adult social care (Needham 2011). One of the government's key policy objectives in promoting personalised care is its commitment to giving people greater choice and control in their lives and defines personalisation as 'the process by which services are tailored to the needs and preferences of citizens. The overall vision is that the state should empower citizens to shape their own lives and the services they receive' (Cabinet Office 2007, p.33). Under these arrangements, people's independence, choice and control in accessing services have largely been operationalised through the use of technologies such as direct payments, individual budgets and self-directed support to purchase their own care and support services from the marketplace. According to some commentators (Gilbert and Powell 2012; Mladenov, Owens and Cribb 2015), this represents a significant transformation from service users being viewed as passive recipients of standardised services to becoming self-managing citizen-consumers and active agents of their own wellbeing. Research by Glendinning *et al.* (2008) on the success of personalisation in improving the lives of service users and carers reported mixed results. While personal budgets afforded flexibility to mental health, learning-disabled and physically disabled service users, older people reported lower levels of satisfaction and greater negative impact on their wellbeing due to the administrative burden involved in managing the budgets (Woolham and Benton 2013). Other research on self-directed support (Homer and Gilder 2008) reported positive evaluations from service users who valued the choice and flexibility that the service offered in promoting independence and wellbeing.

As a policy framework, however, personalisation is not without its critics. Houston (2010), for example, criticises the assumption promoted by personalisation that service users are self-actualising 'consumers' of services within the market who are 'empowered' within a context of consumerism and negative freedom. Other writers (Lymbery 2010) are similarly critical of the policy for being highly individualistic and consumerist in focus which oversimplifies the complexity of human relationships, particularly for those who are physically or cognitively frail and are therefore limited in their ability to exercise choice, such as older people with high support needs. Personalisation can also be viewed as the transfer of risk from the state to the individual, which may result in vulnerable service users being more exposed to various forms of abuse and exploitation (Ferguson 2007; Lymbery and Morley 2012; Ray 2014). One of the key challenges facing practitioners in the implementation of personalisation, therefore, is balancing the promotion of autonomy of service users while providing sufficient protection against exploitation or abuse (Lymbery and Postle 2010).

While social workers are likely to play a central role within personalisation, the nature of their work will arguably become increasingly more administratively focused. Under personalisation, it has been suggested that social workers should spend less time on assessment and more on support, brokerage and advocacy (Department of Health 2008), with statutory agencies undertaking a more enabling role within the personalisation process. Furthermore, as self-assessment by service users is a key feature of the 'co-production' process within personalisation (Needham and Carr 2009), the social work role is likely to concentrate more on facilitating this process. Some commentators however have expressed concern about the apparent marginalisation of the social work role within personalisation:

> on the one hand the apparent aspirations of personalisation are to promote independence and choice, aspirations which are completely congruent with the professional base, yet on the other hand the implication of the policy is to remove social work from the arena of supporting older people to achieve these goals. (Johns 2011, p.131)

While it is likely that social workers will have a continued role in relation to adult safeguarding and other statutory areas of professional practice (Lymbery and Postle 2015), the erosion of their support role and reduced opportunities to contribute to the assessment process may be indicative of a de-professionalisation of the social work role within the personalisation process (Ferguson 2007). Indeed, within the current context of austerity and widespread public service cuts, there is growing evidence of a loss of qualified social workers in adult social care teams and the increased use of unqualified staff to undertake support planning and brokerage tasks within personalisation (Lombard 2011).

Health care social work

Since its inception in the UK at the turn of the twentieth century, hospital social work has played a key role in providing a person-centred and holistic response to the needs of sick and disabled patients and their families at times of transition and crisis. In assisting patients and their families with the social, emotional and economic impacts of ill health, hospital social workers balance the demands of many diverse roles within a multidisciplinary context and provide a sensitive response to acutely ill and vulnerable service users during their period of hospitalisation (Brook and Kitchen 2005). Although much of their work involves responding to the psychosocial needs of patients and families within the discharge-planning process, Australian research (Davis *et al.* 2005) has also highlighted the important liaison and advocacy role hospital social workers undertake with external agencies and organisations. Moreover, in more specialist clinical settings, such as paediatric palliative care and renal units, research from Ireland (Quinn and Clarke 2009, cited in Bywaters, McLeod and Napier 2000) and Israel (Frank, Auslander and Weissgarten 2004) has demonstrated the valuable service social workers provide to distressed parents, patients and families through counselling, advocacy and relationship-based practice within the acute sector. Similarly, in other specialisms such as oncology, haematology, cardiology, neurology, burns and intensive care, hospital social workers as multidisciplinary team members provide important emotional support and family-oriented care to patients and families at times of crisis and transition. However, since the introduction of the community care reforms in the early 1990s in the UK and the move to care management and needs-based assessment, the roles and tasks of the social worker have been radically redefined within an increasingly managerialist organisational culture (Bradley and Manthorpe 2000).

Since the introduction of the new arrangements for assessment and care management in the early 1990s and the shift from a service-led to a needs-led approach to assessment, social workers as care managers are now required to undertake needs and risk assessments, and cost and co-ordinate packages of care within a context of budgetary constraints and service rationing (Lymbery 2005). These arrangements, closely aligned with market principles, represent a major transition in the social work role from providing direct therapeutic work with individuals and families to following narrow and highly routinised assessment protocols within a managerial-technicist approach to needs assessment (Harlow 2003). Furthermore, the emphasis in acute hospitals of increasing patient throughput to make care more efficient and thus avoid delayed discharges has meant that aspects of the 'traditional' social work role, such as counselling and providing emotional support, have become secondary to assessing individual needs and planning for discharge. Research by McLaughlin (2016) found that while hospital social workers provided a sensitive and highly valued service to patients and carers, the highly routinised and administratively driven nature of the care management role in the acute hospital setting significantly diminished their scope for relationship-building, caring and supportive work with patients and families.

Consistent with other UK studies (Beresford, Adshead and Croft 2007), patients and carers appreciated the responsiveness and accessibility of the social work service due to social workers being located within the hospital and valued the social worker's inter-personal and relational skills when they were feeling unwell and emotionally vulnerable.

References

Beresford, P., Adshead, L., and Croft, S. (2007) *Palliative Care, Social Work and Service Users: Making Life Possible.* London: Jessica Kingsley Publishers.

Bogues, S. (2008) *People Work Not Just Paperwork.* Belfast: NISCC.

Boyle, D. (2015) The Roles and Tasks of the Gerontological Social Worker. Ulster University: IRiSS. Available at www.socsci.ulster.ac.uk/irss/2015-boyle.pdf, accessed on 12 February 2017.

Bradley, G. and Manthorpe, J. (eds) (2000) *Working on the Fault Line.* Birmingham: Venture Press.

Brook, J. and Kitchen, A. (2005) 'Social work at the heart of the medical team.' *Social Work in Health Care 40,* 4, 1–18.

Bywaters, P., McLeod, E. and Napier, L. (eds) (2000) *Social Work and Global Health Inequalities: Practice and Policy Developments.* Bristol: Policy Press.

Cabinet Office (2007) *Building on Progress: Public Services.* HM Government Policy Review. London: Cabinet Office.

Carey, M. (2003) 'Anatomy of a care manager.' *Work, Employment and Society 17,* 1, 121–135.

Davis, C., Milosevic, B., Baldry, E. and Walsh, A. (2005) 'Defining the role of the hospital social worker in Australia, part 2: a qualitative approach.' *International Social Work 48,* 3, 289–299.

Department of Health (2007) *Putting People First.* London: Department of Health.

Department of Health (2008) *Transforming Social Care.* London: Department of Health.

Dewane, C. J. (2006) 'Use of self: a primer revisited.' *Clinical Social Work Journal 34,* 4, 543–558.

Dustin, D. (2006) 'Skills and knowledge needed to practice as a care manager: continuity and change.' *Journal of Social Work 6,* 3, 293–313.

Dustin, D. (2012) *The McDonaldization of Social Work.* Aldershot: Ashgate.

Ferguson, I. (2007) 'Increasing user choice or privatising risk? The antinomies of personalisation.' *British Journal of Social Work 37,* 3, 387–403.

Frank, A., Auslander, G. K. and Weissgarten, J. (2004) 'Quality of life of patients with end-stage renal disease at various stages.' *Social Work in Health Care 38,* 2, 1–27.

Gilbert, T. and Powell, J. L. (2012) 'The Place That Social Policy Plays in Shaping the Social Context of Older People.' In M. Davies (ed.) *Social Work with Adults.* Basingstoke: Palgrave Macmillan.

Glendinning, C., Challis, D., Fernandez, J., Jacobs, S., et al. (2008) *Evaluation of the Individual Budgets Pilot Programme: A Final Report.* University of York: SPRU. Available at socialwelfare.bl.uk/subject-areas/services-activity/social-work-care-services/spru/135057IBSEN.pdf, accessed on 12 February 2017.

Harlow, E. (2003) 'New managerialism, social service departments and social work practice today.' *Practice 15*, 2, 29–44.

Harris, J. (2003) *The Social Work Business.* London: Routledge.

Hil, R. (2014, 23 April) 'In defence of social service that puts the need of people first.' *The Conversation*, Griffith University. Available at http://theconversation.com/in-defence-of-social-service-that-puts-the-needs-of-people-first-24568, accessed on 13 December 2016.

Homer, T. and Gilder, P. (2008) *A Review of Self Directed Support in Scotland.* Edinburgh: Scottish Government. Available at www.gov.scot/Publications/2008/05/30134050/0, accessed on 12 February 2017.

Houston, S. (2010) 'Beyond homo economicus: recognition, self-realisation and social work.' *British Journal of Social Work 40*, 3, 841–857.

Johns, R. (2011) *Social Work, Social Policy and Older People.* Exeter: Learning Matters.

Klikauer, T. (2015) 'What is managerialism?' *Critical Sociology 41*, 7–8, 1103–1119.

Lombard, D. (2011) 'Employers "using personalisation to shed social workers".' *Community Care*, 6 April. Available at www.communitycare.co.uk/2011/04/05/employers-using-personalisation-to-shed-social-workers, accessed on 13 December 2016.

Lorenz, W. (2005) 'Decentralisation and social services in England.' *Social Work & Society 3*, 2. Available at www.socwork.net/sws/article/view/191/478, accessed on 3 November 2016.

Lymbery, M. (2005) *Social Work with Older People: Context, Policy and Practice.* London: Sage.

Lymbery, M. (2010) 'A new vision for adult social care? Continuities and change in the care of older people.' *Critical Social Policy 30*, 1, 5–26.

Lymbery, M. and Morley, K. (2012) 'Self-directed support and social work practice.' *Practice: Social Work in Action 24*, 5, 315–327.

Lymbery, M. and Postle, K. (2010) 'Social work in the context of adult social care in England and the resultant implications for social work education.' *British Journal of Social Work 40*, 8, 2502–2522.

Lymbery, M. and Postle, K. (2015) *Social Work and the Transformation of Adult Social Care: Perpetuating a Distorted Vision?* Bristol: Policy Press.

McDonald, A., Postle, K. and Dawson, C. (2007) *Barriers to Retaining and Using Professional Knowledge in Local Authority Social Work Practice with Adults in the UK.* Oxford: Oxford University Press, on behalf of The British Association of Social Workers.

McDonald, C. (2006) 'Institutional transformation: the impact of performance measurement on professional practice in social work.' *Social Work & Society 4*, 1, 25–37.

McLaughlin, J. (2016) 'Social work in acute hospital setting in Northern Ireland: the views of service users, carers and multi-disciplinary professionals.' *Journal of Social Work 16*, 2, 135–154.

Milne, A., Sullivan, M. P., Tanner, D., Richards, S. *et al.* (2014) *Social Work with Older People: A Vision for the Future.* London: The College of Social Work.

Mladenov, T., Owens, J. and Cribb, A. (2015) 'Personalisation in disability services and healthcare: a critical comparative analysis.' *Critical Social Policy 35*, 3, 307–326.

Needham, C. (2011) *Personalising Public Services: Understanding the Personalising Narrative*. Bristol: Policy Press.

Needham, C. and Carr, S. (2009) *Co-Production: An Emerging Evidence Base for Adult Social Care Transformation, Research Briefing 31*. London: Social Care Institute for Excellence.

Payne, M. (2012) *Citizenship Social Work with Older People*. Chicago: Lyceum Books.

Pollitt, C. and Bouckaert, G. (2011) *Public Management Reform: A Comparative Analysis*. Oxford: Oxford University Press.

Postle, K. (2001) 'The social work side is disappearing. I guess it started with us being called care managers.' *Practice 13*, 1, 13–26.

Quinn, S. and Clarke, J. (2009) 'From Research to Policy: Advocacy for Families Caring for Children with Life-Limiting Conditions.' In P. Bywaters, E. McLeod and L. Napier (eds) *Social Work and Global Health Inequalities: Practice and Policy Developments*. Bristol: Policy Press.

Ray, M. (2014) 'Critical Perspectives on Social Work with Older People.' In J. Baars, J. Dohmen, A. Grenier and C. Phillipson (eds) *Ageing, Meaning and Social Structure: Connecting Critical and Humanistic Gerontology*. Bristol: Policy Press.

Ray, M., Bernard, M. and Phillips, J. (2009) *Critical Issues in Social Work with Older People*. Basingstoke: Palgrave Macmillan.

Richards, S. (2000) 'Bridging the divide: elders and the assessment process.' *British Journal of Social Work 30*, 1, 37–49.

Rogowski, S. (2010) *Social Work: The Rise and Fall of a Profession*. Bristol: Policy Press.

Rogowski, S. (2013) *Critical Social Work with Children and Families*. Bristol: Policy Press.

Ruch, G., Turney, D. and Ward, A. (eds) (2010) *Relationship-Based Social Work: Getting to the Heart of Practice*. London: Jessica Kingsley Publishers.

Tanner, D. and Harris, J. (2008) *Working with Older People*. London: Routledge.

Thompson, N. and Thompson, S. (2001) 'Empowering older people: beyond the care model.' *Journal of Social Work 1*, 1, 61–76.

Trevithick, P. (2014) 'Humanising managerialism: reclaiming emotional reasoning, intuition, the relationship and knowledge and skills in social work.' *Journal of Social Work Practice 28*, 3, 287–311.

Tsui, M. and Cheung, F. C. H. (2004) 'Gone with the wind: the impacts of managerialism on human services.' *British Journal of Social Work 34*, 437–442.

Van de Walle, S. and Hammerschmid, G. (2011) 'The impact of the new public management: challenges for coordination and cohesion in European public sectors.' *Halduskultuur – Administrative Culture 12*, 2, 190–209.

Ward, L., Barnes, M. and Gahan, B. (2012) *Well-Being in Old Age: Findings from Participatory Research*. Brighton: Age Concern Brighton/University of Brighton.

Webb, S. (2006) *Social Work in a Risk Society*. Basingstoke: Palgrave Macmillan.

Weinberg, A., Williamson, J., Challis, D. and Hughes, J. (2003) 'What do care managers do? A study of working practice in older people's services.' *British Journal of Social Work 33*, 901–919.

Woolham, J. and Benton, C. (2013) 'The costs and benefits of personal budgets for older people: evidence from a single local authority.' *British Journal of Social Work 43*, 8, 1472–1491.

Chapter 3

RELATIONSHIP-BASED SOCIAL WORK IN FAMILY AND CHILDCARE PRACTICE

James Marshall

One area of social work that could be described as being particularly challenging when using relationship-based social work, would be the broad area of family and childcare, and in particular professionals' practice with parents and carers of children thought to be at risk of neglect or abuse (Ferguson 2011; Trotter 2012). This chapter will concentrate on working with these groups of parents and carers and not the other key areas of family and childcare practice, such as direct work with children, therefore please cross-reference with Chapter 4 on this subject area. This chapter will examine the application of a Relationship-Based Model of social work in working with parents and carers (Doel 2012; Hennessey 2011; Ruch 2005). It will concentrate on the 'engaging' stage of the model (Ruch, Turney, and Ward, 2010), as this is considered a crucial part of developing relationship-based practice. The chapter will review what is meant by the concept of 'partnership', a fundamental component of any relationship-based approach in social work. It will also provide information on some of the challenges faced by social workers working in child protection, and at the end outline a practice example case study of relationship-based social work with parents involved in the child protection system. This discussion on the child protection challenges is based on inquiry findings and research (Broadhurst *et al.* 2010; Harker 2016; Munro 2011) and my own practice experience as an independent social worker in Northern Ireland. Finally, this chapter will also examine the research on the skills required by practitioners in relationship-based work in family and childcare practice, and make the case for extending this as a method of working in child protection cases.

The child protection context for practice

Family and childcare social work is a complex area of practice and the perceived failings are consistently in the public domain (Brandon *et al.* 2010; Devaney *et al.* 2013; Ruch *et al.* 2010). The lessons from child protection inquiries and 'serious case reviews' (SCRs) in England (Laming 2003; Munro 2011), and their equivalent in Northern Ireland, 'case management reviews' (CMRs) (Devaney *et al.* 2013), all suggest, with the benefit of hindsight, that social work practices can be improved in relation to the risk assessment of parents and the safeguarding of vulnerable children, and they stress the importance of social workers having effective relationships with parents and their children. This chapter will concentrate on this area of 'child protection', sometimes also referred to in policies as 'safeguarding'. Although these terms are often used interchangeably in the literature they are very different concepts in practice, both legally and procedurally. The 'child protection' phrase denotes statutory social work intervention and investigation due to allegations of child abuse and neglect of children by parents, carers and others, whereas 'safeguarding' is a much broader concept that advocates preventative social work practice and implies that for some of these types of referrals a family support approach may be more appropriate than a child protection reaction (Department for Education 2015; Department of Health 2016). Parents subjected to a child protection investigation will obviously have very different experiences of social services compared to those being offered a family support service (Spratt and Callan 2004). In statutory family and childcare social work, the legal mandate for investigating child abuse is 'significant harm' (Children Act 1989 and Children (NI) Order 1995), and it can be used to justify what could be construed as the imposition of a social work service on parents, if there is a 'reasonable cause' to suspect their children may be at risk of significant harm.

The investigation of child abuse in the UK has for decades been a controversial public issue. Between 2002 and 2016 the demand on child protection services has shown an 88 per cent increase in the number of children subject to a child protection plan in the UK (National Society for the Prevention of Cruelty to Children 2015).

This has been attributed to a number of factors, including the effect of the Victoria Climbié (Laming 2003) and Baby Peter Connelly (Laming 2009) child death tragedies, and their aforementioned inquiries; a greater awareness of the impact of domestic violence and neglect on children; and some high-profile 'child sexual exploitation' (CSE) criminal trials and inquiries (Marshall 2014; Rochdale Borough Safeguarding Children Board 2013).

This surge in child protection referrals and the subsequent increase in risk assessment activity (House of Commons 2015) has obviously presented a major challenge for already hard-pressed frontline child protection social workers. The argument could be made that such an increase in practitioners' workloads, during a lengthy period of austerity and reduced spending in public services, has produced a more functional, technical and procedurally driven method of working with families (Bilson and Martin 2016; Ruch *et al.* 2010). These demands could naturally reduce the amount of time social work practitioners have to develop a more partnership-type approach or relationship-based engagement with parents (Parton 2011). It begs the question: do these pressures on social workers in cases such as Daniel Pelka (Coventry Children Safeguarding Board 2013) mean they don't have sufficient assessment time to enable them to really build up relationships and get to know the parent and child and wider family relationships? Even if they had the time, what would be the prospect of relationship-based social working when the parents and carers are very resistant (Marshall 2011). The challenge of 'partnership working' with non-compliant or obstructive parents and carers will be dealt with in some detail later in this chapter.

Based on research (Dale 2004; Holland and Scourfield 2004; Parton 1991) and my own practice experience, the issue of relationship-based social work in statutory family and childcare social work is often embroiled in the debate on the use of authority and legal powers to control and manage a child protection investigation. The issues are of competing legal rights, such as the parents' right to a private and family life (Human Rights Act 1998, article 8), and children's rights under the UN Convention on the Rights of the Child (1989) to be protected from abuse or ill-treatment. Social services' respective statutory safeguarding responsibilities under UK legislation, such as the Children Act (1989) or the Children (NI) Order (1995), place social workers in an invidious position of having to manage potentially competing rights on a daily basis when deciding when, and how, they can intervene in family life (Parton 2011).

The guiding legal principles of childcare and human rights legislation throughout the UK do suggest an implicit duty on social workers to work in 'partnership' and to support parents; included in this is the duty to provide family support services. The legal aspiration contained in the family support requirement presumes the full involvement of parents and children in decisions about their family life, but this aspiration has been met with some scepticism by various commentators (Barlow and Scott 2010; Hayes and Spratt 2009; Parton 2011; Thorburn, Lewis and Shemmings 1995). On the one hand the principles underlying the respective legislation, including the 'welfare check list', were aimed at reducing the amount of state involvement in family life and increasing parental and children's rights in family law, but others (McKeigue and Beckett 2004) use indicators such as legal delays and an increase in the number of care orders granted (House of Commons 2015) to suggest that the trend is for more state involvement in family life, rather than less. By the end of March 2015 a total of 69,540 children were 'looked after' by local authorities in England, with just over 42,000 of these being as a result of legal care orders, and a similar increase has been noted in the other UK countries. The total number of children looked after has increased steadily in England over the past seven years and in fact is now higher than at any point since 1985. The potential 'refocusing debate' policy (Cleaver and Walker 2004; Parton 2011), summarised as the need for social services to become focused more on preventative services than child protection investigations, would appear not to have been realised (Bilson and Martin 2016; Cleaver and Walker 2004; Hayes and Spratt 2014; Platt 2006).

The dual role for social workers, to support parents and yet on other occasions investigate possible significant harm (Cleaver and Freeman 1995; Hayes and Spratt 2014; Munro 2008), will of course produce professional dilemmas in practice for social workers as the roles are not mutually exclusive. It poses issues for parents who wonder if you are there to support them or investigate them – in reality you are often doing both simultaneously, which is not the best basis for relationship-based social work.

This dichotomy of roles does raise some important issues, such as how social workers can possibly engage in an effective manner with parents, some of whom may be deliberately abusing or neglecting their children. Laming (2009) and Munro (2011) clearly outline in their reviews the stark reality that a social worker's relationship with some parents can be characterised by the parents attempting to deliberately deceive the authorities, including social services. This has obviously been the case in many child abuse reviews (Coventry Children Safeguarding Board 2013; Windsor and Maidenhead Local Safeguarding Board 2014). Unfortunately some parents can also be overtly verbally and physically aggressive and resistant to social work involvement (Littlechild 2005; Trotter 2012). In other instances this perceived non-co-operation or resistant behaviour (Forester, Westlake and Glynn 2012; Marshall 2011) can be more subtle and may be due to other associated factors such as parental substance misuse, mental health issues or perhaps a parent with a learning disability. Whilst these types of factors can certainly limit parenting capacity, they also cannot be underestimated in limiting the application of a Relationship-Based Model in child protection social work.

Is partnership with parents compatible with child protection social work?

Any social work practitioner will know that child protection work is characterised by risk assessment and protection planning; they frequently use models primarily based on ecological social work theories, such as the Common Assessment Framework (CAF) (Department for Education and Skills 2006) or, in Northern Ireland, the Understanding the Needs of Children in Northern Ireland (UNOCINI) framework (DHSSPS 2008). These ecological approaches and models assume that the social worker (and other professionals involved) will assess the child within their family and community context (Bronfenbrenner 1992; DHSSPS 2008; Horwath and Morrison 2001). In order to understand the child's world, the social worker must get close not just to them but also to their parents and significant others, who have or may have a caring role in the future. A key component of all the assessment models used in the UK is the social worker's ability to assess 'parenting capacity', usually by adopting a strengths and deficits approach. This ability to work with parents is essential to assess their understandings and perceptions of the child protection issue. Munro (2011) emphasises the point that any method of intervention used with parents requires the social worker 'to be able to engage and form a trusting relationship with the child and family members' (p.45). This is important for a number of reasons: first, most children at risk will continue to live with their primary carers, usually parents; and second, even when their children are 'looked after' by the state, parents continue to play a key role in their children's lives and reasonable contact is presumed in law (Children (NI) Order 1995).

However, most assessment models, CAF (2006) and UNOCINI (2008), for example, whilst placing some emphasis on the importance of working in 'partnership' with parents and carers, do not place any great emphasis on the importance of the social worker–parent relationship as a means of improving partnership and thus possibly increasing the veracity of any risk assessment. The much-used word 'partnership' is prominent in all child protection policies, Working Together to Safeguard Children (HM Government 2010) and Cooperating to Safeguard Children (Department of Health 2016), and usually implies a good working relationship between the professional and the service user, such as a parent involved with a child protection investigation. Partnership as a concept suggests a shared understanding of goals and power between the parties, and not just co-operation. Since the common focus and primary concern in child protection work is the child, then it is presumed that to work in partnership the parent and social worker will have an agreed understanding of the child's needs, parenting responsibilities and any 'significant harm' risks. This can be a problem in practice as there may be little or no agreement between the parent and the social worker on these frequently contested concepts. These could include the challenge of the professional and parent agreeing on what is 'good enough' parenting, and what are a child's developmental (and other) needs. Also, what are the risks posed by family issues such as substance misuse, domestic violence and the impact on parenting of societal issues such as poverty and deprivation?

In child protection practice the power relationship can also present major challenges for partnership working (Parton 1998). The parent usually still retains their 'parental responsibility' for their child and, with it, their associated powers and duties under our respective legislation such as the Children (NI) Order, article 5. But in many child protection cases the parents may feel that the rights fulcrum is tilted in favour of the state and the power of social services. Parents often feel they have little power in such situations because of their immediate worry and concerns about their children being removed from their care and the powers of the family courts (Calder 2008; Cleaver and Freeman 1995). It has been argued (Dale 2004) that the partnership concept can be used against parents as they are not given many options in these situations, and any challenges they present may be construed as them being 'unco-operative' clients (Ferguson 2011). Participation in the assessment process, as it's often on a non-voluntary basis, can itself be problematic for parents, as Petrie (2007) suggests: 'Embarking on forms of participation primarily to meet agency expectations, rather than engaging on individualised and dynamic relationships with children and their families, merely offers tokenistic partnership that can be experienced by service users as unhelpful' (p.378).

Childcare services and social workers can have good reason to want to take control of situations where a child is deemed to be at risk, and the procedural environment in which they work, even more so post-Laming (2003 and 2009), lends itself to them thinking they have to take control. In an era of increasing numbers of forensic-type child protection risk assessments being undertaken, especially on younger children, Bilson and Martin's (2016) research concludes that there is 'little evidence to support this scale of statutory involvement' (p.12), their argument being that an increasing number of young families are being unnecessarily drawn into the 'child protection net' at the expense of more effective early years preventative services.

The research on parental participation seems to support this argument (Dale 2004; Hayes and Spratt 2014; Platt 2006; Spratt and Callan 2004) as parents experienced social workers to be solely risk-focused and reluctant to recognise any parental strengths and their relationships with their children. Partnership with parents could be characterised by 'full' participation in the process and having shared goals, involvement in decision-making forums and the development of a trusting relationship. An increased use of signed contracts with parents, parental attendance at child protection case conferences, 'looked after' children reviews and other core group meetings can be construed as evidence of a more participatory, partnership approach being promoted by social workers. But the research (Cleaver and Freeman 1995; National Children's Bureau 2016) suggests that parents rarely felt they were 'equal' partners in these processes and that they can rarely influence the decisions being made by social workers and other professionals about their children. Petrie (2007) says that one of the reasons for this deficit is that 'the formal aspects of partnership have little impact on the recipients of child protection interventions: it is the quality of the parent's relationship with the worker involved that is important and empowering' (p.378).

Research would suggest that parents appreciate full involvement and participation when decisions are being considered about their children, and they want honesty about the nature of the power relationship that exists between themselves and social workers (Dale 2004; Holland 2000; Spratt and Callan 2004). There may be resistance on the part of social workers to fully acknowledge the legal powers (or perceived powers) that they have, in the parent's mind. Being honest about the power dynamic and ensuring parents know their rights should be a cornerstone of any relationship-based working with parents in child protection work. At times a differentiation needs to be made about each parent, for instance, if one is assessed as being a risk to children, and the other is deemed to be the 'non-abusing' or protective parent. The 'safe parent' may well be placed under considerable pressure to choose between their partner and their parental safeguarding role in respect of their children (Petrie 2007). Also, other relatives may become key safeguarding figures when it comes to child protection, and relatives and other carers may also be considered when considering the Relationship Model of practice. One manifestation of this has been the development over two decades of a family group conference model in the UK; this process involves extended family members and others in safeguarding and caring for children who may otherwise end up in state care (Connolly 2006; Hayes 2000). Family group conferences are resource intensive but have a good track record of increasing kinship care and producing effective child protection practice.

Relationship-based theory and child protection practice

Historically social work has been professionally characterised as a humanistic occupation where the desire to help people has been inextricably linked to the development of a therapeutic relationship (Howe 2008; Sudberry 2002). It could be argued that this foundation for the profession has been eroded over the decades with the growth of 'managerialism' in social work agencies, target-based services and time-limited assessment processes. Murphy, Duggan and Joseph (2013) are sceptical as to whether the relationship-based social work model can be applied to all areas of social work practice:

> The role of, and the extent to which, the relationship between the social worker and service user is considered to be directly responsible for change is dependent upon the theoretical underpinnings that inform the nature and scope of the helping relationship. Simply to suggest, however, that the whole repertoire of approaches to social work and the multiple practice contexts in which social work is carried out can together be reducible to a coherent generic description as a 'relationship based approach' is too broad a generalisation. (p.705)

Social workers' child protection involvement with parents is frequently short term in nature, with cases being closed quickly following a very short initial assessment period.[1] Combined with increasing workloads and referral rates, the social worker's opportunities to develop a meaningful relationship with parents and/or their children in family and childcare practice are extremely limited, and yet, as we have seen, this relationship has often been deemed crucial, especially for practice with reluctant service users. The importance of relationship-based work in family and childcare practice seems crucial, even for parents deemed to be 'unco-operative'.

> A recent overview of the evidence about effective interventions for complex families, where there were concerns about (or evidence of) a child suffering significant harm, showed the importance of providing 'a dependable professional relationship' for parents and children, in particular with those families who conceal or minimise their difficulties. (Barlow and Scott 2010, p.24)

Based on this, there does seem to be place for a relationship-based approach in practice with parents but a purist 'person-centred approach' (Trevethick 2003) is rarely achievable as the parents are frequently involuntary service users. Murphy *et al.* (2013) assert that true relationship-based social work with parents in child protection practice is not achievable, as the relationship cannot be fully person-centred, and it is usually just a means to bring about forced changes in

---

1   Initial assessments under UNOCINI (2008) in Northern Ireland have to be completed within ten working days; some of the CAF (2006) requirements (England and Wales) have been extended following the Munro (2011) review.

parental behaviour and attitudes and thus safeguard a child. Murphy *et al.* (2013) go on to state:

> However, we would argue that, even when this is the case, this does not reduce the instrumental nature of these relationships. In person-centred practice, there is no instrumental element to the relationship. By definition, when an instrumental aspect is introduced into the relationship, it is no longer person-centred in the technical sense of this term. As such, it is difficult to see how social workers can, in the true sense of the meaning, consider themselves to be person-centred. (p.715)

The challenge for social work then seems to be how to bridge this gap when applying a relationship-based model to work with parents involved with the child protection system.

Application of a Relationship Model with parents in child protection work

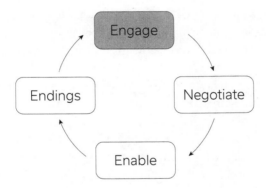

In this section we need to consider the application of the '4 Stage Relationship-Based Model' in family and childcare practice. In practice social workers are *engaging* with parents and carers, *negotiating* with parents and carers, *enabling* change using the model and finally *ending* the relationship (Hennessey 2011; Ruch *et al.* 2010). Based on research (Bilson and Martin 2016; Munro 2008) and my own practice experience, a key stage of developing any relationship is the referral, first contact or engaging stage of the process with parents and their children. It is this *engaging stage* that this chapter will concentrate on, as a good start is deemed essential in developing any relationship-based social work.

In family and childcare protection practice, social workers are often deemed to be imposing a service on a parent rather than it being requested. It could be argued it is a forced relationship, and the initial parameters for the engagement need to be made as transparent as possible. At the referral stage and subsequent initial assessment stage, if an allegation is about potential abuse or neglect, social workers are naturally often suspicious of parents. This is understandable and social workers have to be discerning and focused on the needs of the children in the family. However, the safeguarding responsibility that social workers have should not preclude the development of an effective relationship with parents, and this could enhance safeguarding as a result (Barlow and Scott 2010). Aside from the children themselves, if of sufficient age, the parents are generally the main sources of information about family life. It is therefore vital that social workers focus on engaging with them and developing a relationship with parents from when the referral is received.

At the initial stage, referrals can come from a variety of sources, including anonymous allegations of abuse or neglect. The challenge for social workers in managing the information received is that it can have limited details, be confusing about the levels of risk to the children and the referrer may not want to be identified as the source of the information (Hayes and Spratt 2014; Thorpe and Bilson 1998). This can set an immediate challenge for social workers wanting to develop relationship-based practice with a parent, as they cannot disclose all the information they have. From the outset social work practitioners are mindful of the parent's human rights, including their right to private and family life (Human Rights Act 1998, article 8) but they will balance this with their duty to protect children.

The challenge in family and childcare practice is knowing how to engage in a respectful and honest way with parents and at the same time retain some professional detachment to inform your professional risk assessment. Ferguson (2011) thought social workers should presume conflict with parents in such initial encounters, and this potential for conflict and the power differential in a child protection situation need to be openly stated and managed. The engagement stage of a relationship-based model (Hennessey 2011; Ruch 2005) presumes that normally this initial contact and assessment stage will be characterised by the principles of openness, trust, respect, choice and self-determination in the social worker–service user interaction. In a child protection initial assessment the engagement may well be characterised by mistrust, limited choice, little respect and guarded openness.

At the initial stages of an investigation social workers should ensure parents are made aware of their legal rights and responsibilities and their options in relation to engaging with social services at this juncture. Written information is always advisable, as parents may be in shock or crisis mode and may not fully comprehend or understand any verbal information or advice given. It would be empowering for parents to be made aware of the legal mandate and procedural guidance under which social workers got involved in their family life, again in written form if possible, supported by simple explanations of course. Parents in child protection cases generally seem to appreciate as much honesty as possible from the professionals involved with their family (Ferguson 2011; Trotter 2012) yet there may be reluctance from anxious social workers to disclose any information in case it compromises their investigations. Measures need to be considered to improve this level of honesty between all parties and build a foundation for relationship-based work. The use of the aforementioned written contract for the engagement stage could be beneficial as it can outline what is negotiable (and what is not) at this stage. As stated, parents are generally an invaluable source of information on their children and in any assessment their increased involvement in the process will usually facilitate better assessments and relationship-based working (Dale 2004; Forrester *et al.* 2012).

Child protection case study

The following is based on a real family and childcare case, but adapted to respect confidentiality issues. It outlines key issues for engagement with parents and key points for social workers in starting to build a relationship during a child protection investigation.

The referral concerned Ms B and her children – C, her five-year-old son, and D, her 18-month-old daughter. The anonymous caller alleged that Ms B was drinking 'every night and taking legal highs'; as a result he claimed that the children were being 'neglected' and C was rarely at school, and said 'you need to check up on her'. He also claimed Ms B's new partner was violent to her and the children had witnessed this. The caller did not want to be identified or give his name but left a mobile number in case the social worker wanted to contact him again.

An initial check on the office computer records showed that Ms B was first known to social services two years ago because of allegations that her then male partner (Mr B) was a drug dealer and was abusive to her during her pregnancy. Mr B has contact with the two children every second weekend under a court contact order. More recently Ms B has asked at the office for financial help twice in the past eight months and asked for a report so she can be rehoused from her current flat because of antisocial behaviour in the area.

On the day of the referral Ms B was contacted by a social worker; Ms B thought it was about her housing and financial problems, and she got very angry when the social worker told her it was about child protection allegations and could not tell her who made the referral. Ms B commented, in colourful language, 'It's probably my (ex-partner) as he's threatened me with social services if I don't stop asking him for maintenance money.' Ms B denies any problems with drinking or taking drugs and did not present as being on any substances. She says the social worker can check her son's (C) school attendance and her GP (general practitioner) records but that's as far as it goes. She asks the social worker to leave and not come back unless she is 'offering her help or has a court order'!

When the social worker checks with the school, C's attendance is at the 75 per cent level and his presentation and application in school is 'normal'. The GP says that she cannot share information unless Ms B gives written permission; the social worker persists and says the enquiry is part of a child protection investigation and then the GP says there has been no evidence of addictions on Ms B's medical records. But she had been in the surgery last month looking for contraceptive advice and D was given an immunisation that was overdue.

The key issues of engagement and relationship-based social work with Ms B and the family are listed in Table 3.1 (please note the case was more complex than this and these three pathways are for illustrative purposes).

Table 3.1 Case study: Pathway engagement options

1. Full relationship-based engagement approach	2. Engagement to assess risk to the children only	3. Child protection relationship-based engagement
The initial referrer is contacted for additional information and asked if he is Mr B (he was Ms B's ex-partner).	The initial referrer is advised to keep telling social services if he has concerns and especially at the time when he has evidence the children may be at risk.	The referrer is told that the social worker thinks he may be an ex-partner and if he allows his name to be used this will ensure better safeguarding of the children in the future.
Ms B is informed who the referral was from and given all the details so she can give her views on each allegation.	Ms B is told in the next visit that she must allow the social worker access to her home, or a court order would be applied for.	Ms B is told who social workers think the referrer may be but this detail will only be disclosed as a part of a signed 'safety in partnership' agreement.
Ms B is then offered a choice whether she wants a social worker to call again and about the type of services she wants from social services; a written contract may be agreed and signed.	Ms B is told that this is a child protection investigation and assessment and that her co-operation is required to avoid any more statutory intervention in her life; she is advised to see a solicitor as soon as possible.	Ms B is asked to work in partnership with social services and is asked to identify the needs of her children and any help or assistance that she requires. The social worker offers to help with the housing issues and financial matters if future access to the home (at agreed times) is guaranteed.

Please also note that the three pathways are not mutually exclusive but based on research and professional experience, the third pathway 'Child protection relationship-based engagement' would appear to be the one with the best chance of successfully engaging with parents whilst still undertaking the child protection social work (Dale 2004; Forrester *et al.* 2012; Holland 2000). There would appear to be no reason for social workers not to at least attempt this third approach first to facilitate the building of a relationship (Petrie 2007; Ruch *et al.* 2010).

The potential for a more meaningful engagement from Ms B and Mr B in the assessment process and enhanced safeguarding practice could be the result (Broadhurst *et al.* 2010; Ferguson 2011; Taylor 2011). If the relationship-based engagement approach was not working with a parent, the social worker could of course then revert to a more 'risk to children engagement' strategy and take more control over the situation.

References

Barlow, J. and Scott, J. (2010) *Safeguarding in the 21st Century – Where to Now.* Dartington: Research in Practice.

Bilson, A. and Martin, K. (2016) 'Referrals and child protection in England: one in five children referred to children's services and one in nineteen investigated before the age of five.' *British Journal of Social Work.* Available at http://bjsw.oxfordjournals.org/content/early/2016/05/19/bjsw.bcw054.full, accessed on 4 November 2016.

Brandon, M., Sidebottom, P., Bailey, S. and Belderson, P. (2010) *A Study of Recommendations Arising from Serious Case Review 2009–2010.* Research Report DFE-RR157. London: Department of Education.

Broadhurst, K., Wastell, D., White, S., Hall, C. *et al.* (2010) 'Performing "initial assessment": identifying the latent conditions for error at the front-door of local authority children's services.' *British Journal of Social Work 40,* 2, 352–370.

Bronfenbrenner, U. (1992) *Ecological Systems Theory.* London: Jessica Kingsley Publishers.

Calder, M. (2008) *Contemporary Risk Assessment in Safeguarding Children.* Lyme Regis: Russell House Publishing.

Cleaver, H. and Freeman, P. (1995) *Parental Perspective in Cases of Suspected Child Abuse.* London: HMSO.

Cleaver, H. and Walker, S. (2004) 'From policy to practice: the implementation of a new framework for social work assessments of children and families.' *Children and Family Social Work 9,* 1, 81–90.

Connolly, M. (2006) 'Fifteen years of family group conferencing: coordinators talk about their experiences in Aotearoa New Zealand.' *British Journal of Social Work 36,* 4, 523–540.

Coventry Children Safeguarding Board (2013) *Serious Case Review: Daniel Pelka.* Coventry: LSCB.

Dale, P. (2004) '"Like fish in a bowl": parents' perceptions of child protection services.' *Child Abuse Review 13,* 137–157.

Department for Education (2015) *Working Together to Safeguard Children: Statutory Guidance on Inter-Agency Working to Safeguard and Promote the Welfare of Children.* London: HMSO.

Department for Education and Skills (2006) *Common Assessment for Children and Young People.* London: Stationery Office.

Department of Health (2016) *Co-operating to Safeguard Children and Young People in Northern Ireland.* Belfast: DOH.

Department of Health Social Services and Public Safety (2008) *Understanding the Needs of Children in Northern Ireland Guidance.* Belfast: DHSSPS.

Devaney, J., Bunting, L., Hayes, D. and Lazenblatt, A. (2013) *Translating the Learning into Action: An Overview of Learning Arising from Case Management Reviews in Northern Ireland 2003–2008.* Belfast: DHSSPS, QUB, NSPCC.

Doel, M. (2012) *Social Work: The Basics*. London: Routledge.

Ferguson, H. (2011) *Child Protection Practice*. Basingstoke: Palgrave Macmillan.

Forrester, D., Westlake, D. and Glynn, G. (2012) 'Parental resistance and social worker skills: towards a theory of motivational social work.' *Child & Family Social Work 17*, 118–129.

Harker, L. (2016) *Demand Management as the Driver for Reforming Child Protection Services*. London: NCB.

Hayes, D. (2000) 'The use of family group conferences in child protection work: an exploration of professionals' views.' *Childcare in Practice 6*, 2, 124–146.

Hayes, D. and Spratt, T. (2009) 'Child welfare interventions: patterns of social work practice.' *British Journal of Social Work 39*, 8, 1575–1597.

Hayes, D. and Spratt, T. (2014) 'Child welfare as child protection then and now: what social workers did and continue to do.' *British Journal of Social Work 44*, 3, 615–635.

Hennessey, R. (2011) *Relationship Skills in Social Work*. London: Sage.

HM Government (2010) *Working Together to Safeguard Children: A Guide to Inter-Agency Working to Safeguard and Promote the Welfare of Children*. London: Department for Children, Schools and Families.

Holland, S. (2000) 'The assessment relationship: interactions between social workers and parents in child protection assessments.' *British Journal of Social Work 30*, 2, 149–163.

Holland, S. and Scourfield, J. (2004) 'Liberty and respect in child protection.' *British Journal of Social Work 34*, 21–36.

Horwath, J. and Morrison, T. (2001) 'The Assessment of Parental Motivation to Change.' In J. Horwath (ed.) *The Child's World: Assessing Children in Need*. London: Jessica Kingsley Publishers.

House of Commons (2015) *Briefing Paper 04470: Children in Care England Statistics*. London: House of Commons Library.

Howe, D. (2008) *The Emotionally Intelligent Social Worker*. Basingstoke: Palgrave Macmillan.

Laming, Lord (2003) *The Victoria Climbié Inquiry*. London: HMSO.

Laming, Lord (2009) *The Protection of Children in England: A Progress Report*. London: Stationery Office.

Littlechild, B. (2005) 'The stresses arising from violence, threats and aggression against child protection social workers.' *Journal of Social Work 5*, 61–82.

Marshall, J. (2011) 'Assessing the Risk to Children Despite Parental Resistance.' In B. Taylor (ed.) *Working with Aggression and Resistance in Social Work*. Exeter: Learning Matters.

Marshall, K. (2014) *Child Sexual Exploitation in Northern Ireland: Report of the Independent Inquiry*. Belfast: Criminal Justice Inspection, RQIA.

McKeigue, B. and Beckett, C. (2004) 'Care proceedings under the 1989 Children Act: rhetoric and reality.' *British Journal of Social Work 34*, 831–849.

Munro, E. (2008) *Effective Child Protection*. London: Sage.

Munro, E. (2011) *The Munro Review of Child Protection: Final Report: A Child-Centred System*. London: Stationery Office.

Murphy, D., Duggan, M. and Joseph, S. (2013) 'Relationship-based social work and its compatibility with the person-centred approach: principled versus instrumental perspectives.' *British Journal of Social Work 43*, 703–719.

National Children's Bureau (2016) *Rethinking Children's Services: Fit for the Future*. London: NCB.

National Society for the Prevention of Cruelty to Children (2015) *How Safe are Our Children? 2015*. London: NSPCC.

Parton, N. (1991) *Governing the Family: Childcare, Child Protection and the State.* Basingstoke: Macmillan.

Parton, N. (1998) 'Risk, advanced liberalism and child welfare: the need to rediscover uncertainty and ambiguity.' *British Journal of Social Work 28,* 1, 5–27.

Parton, N. (2011) 'Child protection and safeguarding in England: changing and competing conceptions of risk and their implications for social work.' *British Journal of Social Work 41,* 5, 854–875.

Petrie, S. (2007) 'Partnership with Parents.' In K. Wilson and A. James (eds) *The Child Protection Handbook: The Practitioner's Guide to Safeguarding Children.* Edinburgh: Bailliere Tindall Elsevier.

Platt, D. (2006) 'Investigation or initial assessment of child concerns? The impact of the refocusing initiative on social work practice.' *British Journal of Social Work 36,* 2, 267–281.

Rochdale Borough Safeguarding Children Board (2013) *The Overview Report of the Serious Case Review in Respect of Young People.* Rochdale: RBSCB.

Ruch, G. (2005) 'Relationship-based practice and reflective practice: holistic approaches to contemporary childcare social work.' *Child & Family Social Work 10,* 2, 111–123.

Ruch, G., Turney, D. and Ward, A. (2010) *Relationship-Based Social Work: Getting to the Heart of Practice.* London: Jessica Kingsley Publishers.

Spratt, T. and Callan, J. (2004) 'Parent's views on social work interventions in child welfare cases.' *British Journal of Social Work 34,* 199–224.

Sudberry, J. (2002) 'Key features of therapeutic social work: the use of relationship.' *Journal of Social Work Practice 16,* 2, 149–161.

Taylor, B. J. (2011) *Working with Aggression and Resistance in Social Work.* Exeter: Learning Matters.

Thorburn, J., Lewis, A. and Shemmings, D. (1995) *Paternalism or Partnership? Family Involvement in the Child Protection Process.* London: HMSO.

Thorpe, D. and Bilson, A. (1998) 'From protection to concern: child protection careers without apologies.' *Children and Society 12,* 373–386.

Trevethick, P. (2003) 'Effective relationship-based practice: a theoretical exploration.' *Journal of Social Work Practice 17,* 2, 163–178.

Trotter, C. (2012) *Working with Involuntary Clients.* London: Sage.

United Nations (1989) *The United Nations Convention on the Rights of the Child.* New York: United Nations.

Windsor and Maidenhead Local Safeguarding Board (2014) *Serious Case Review: Callum Wilson.* Windsor: LSCB.

Chapter 4

BUILDING RELATIONSHIPS WITH YOUNG PEOPLE

Cheryl McMullin

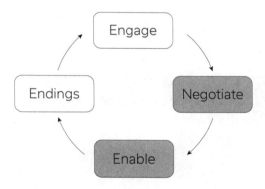

This chapter will discuss the importance of building relationships with young people along with a case study and focusing mainly on the application of two components of the 4 Stage Relationship Model; those chosen are *Negotiate* and *Enable*. There will be a focus on 'looked after' young people as they are a particular group most likely to have had many professionals, in particular social work intervention, in their lives. Some young people have experienced numerous interventions from many social work teams, for example, an initial assessment team at referral stage right through to leaving and after-care social workers. A young person may have had a number of social work practitioners and Winter (2015) highlights that continuous changes in their social worker can become a barrier to building positive relationships, especially when children have experienced trauma, the reasons for this having been explored in Chapter 1.

I have worked extensively with young people and have been lucky to meet some of the most clever, talented and resilient who have overcome adversity and the challenges of the care system. I have also met many other young people who have struggled and at times been disadvantaged with some of the limitations of organisations and professionals trying to support them, for example, multiple changes in practitioner, increased caseloads and fewer contact hours spent with young people. In my experience working relationships with young people became incredibly important even if at times the social work intervention was not initially welcome. I was always impressed when many young people demonstrated excellent perception skills and could tell if an adult or 'professional' was being genuine or not. Winter (2015) suggests that children desire better relationships with their social workers. I think children and young people need warm and authentic adults who might not have all the answers or resources but essentially do care; this can only be achieved through relational work.

Current context: challenging times

Children and young people are important as they are the next generation and like other vulnerable groups are not fully valued or protected in society. The care and protection of children in particular has been highlighted in the media, which often evidences poor practice with fatal consequences, for example, Peter Connelly (2008) and Daniel Pelka (2012). Thompson and Thompson (2008) highlight that the media plays a significant part in how social work is perceived in society and simplifies complicated social work issues This, coupled with increased political and socio-economic issues, compounds the problems faced by family and childcare social work. Key issues for consideration are themes such as poverty, substance misuse/addiction, criminality, mental and/or other health issues, education/unemployment, domestic abuse, sectarianism, racism and single parent families. If children have experienced or are experiencing some of these issues it will undoubtedly make relational work more challenging. Young people may find trusting adults more difficult and often misunderstand well-meaning social work relationships and good intentions or interventions.

Family and childcare social work is one of the most complex areas of work; Munro (2011) highlights that child protection work involves working with uncertainty. Paradoxically it can often be the place where many newly qualified social workers enter into their first employment because of vacancies due to traditionally high staff turnover. Family and childcare can often lose experienced and skilled staff owing to the complexity of work and increased caseloads. Many organisations may employ short-term agency workers and contracts; this can have implications for relational work because the agency worker may not know how long they will be available and the permanency principle for 'looked after' children is compromised as a result.

McCarthy (2015) highlights the stress and pressure social workers feel under and that there is evidence to suggest it is not a long-term career choice, in fact anywhere between 8 and 13 years in research by Curtis, Moriarty and Netten (2009). When working with a vulnerable group like children in the care system and understanding their experience of abuse, practitioners themselves may also experience secondary trauma. Sometimes it is exceptionally difficult to share, listen or understand the lived experience of someone else's abuse if practitioners are not aware or well supported themselves, and they may experience 'compassion fatigue' (McFadden, Campbell and Taylor 2014).

What is commonly referred to as 'burn out' among professionals can be attributed to factors such as poor professional supervision and support, complexity of work, managing resistance and large caseloads. Research by Galek *et al.* (2011) describes three elements: emotional exhaustion, feeling ineffective and becoming emotionally distant. Turbett (2014) also discusses social work 'burn out' and practitioners feeling ineffective about their interventions and having doubts in relation to their ability and competence. If a practitioner is experiencing these feelings over a sustained period of time then this will greatly impact on the quality of relationships with the young people and their families.

Working with children and intrinsic motivation

There needs to be some reflection on and consideration of how difficult the work can be and this necessitates the need for high-quality supervision and a good supervisory relationship (Wonnacott 2012). All practitioners have experienced childhood and issues may often resonate with practitioners. It is important that practitioners develop increased self-awareness and self-knowledge when working with children and young people and consider their own motivations for working in this setting. Young people often say it is your 'job' or

'You get paid to do this', and it is the caring aspect of the profession that needs to be reinforced and the practitioner's intrinsic motivation for the work.

Engaging in the spaces and places

When working with children we need to take into account the spaces and places where we carry out relational work and whether or not the environment is conducive to enhance this. When considering work with children and families, Ferguson (2014) highlights the challenges of the work environment and practitioners being aware of the places where they carry out direct work. Practitioners should not overlook simple things that might have an impact on engaging, for example, the effects that smell, chaos, cleanliness or dogs/pets may have on the senses (Ferguson 2014). We need to be creative and think about where is the best place for the work and be honest about the impact of these experiences.

Even the practical arrangements need some consideration, for example, timing of appointments, location and driving distances. Some work can take place in a police station, hospital, court or in custody, locations that can sometimes be alien and intimidating. 'Looked after' children in residential care often have not only residential social workers but also community-based practitioners coming in and out of what is essentially their home and safe space.

When engaging with children we need to be aware of our 'professional style', for example, the way we present ourselves and communicate. Koprowska (2010) highlights phatic communication as a more conversational style of talking which is non-threatening, such as talking about football results or music festivals. This type of non-threatening communication is extremely effective in building relationships, especially with children when trying to relate and see the world from their perspective. Damour (2016) advises that teenagers do not welcome direct questions or those that are pursuing a certain angle. Furthermore, teenagers find that if someone is rushed, not really listening or have good reasons for asking the questions it can be a source of annoyance. Practitioners need to consider factors like the place, suitability and timing; for example, is the practitioner rushing to another appointment? Often the best work I engaged in with young people was in a more conversational and non-direct approach, such as making a cup of tea, completing a piece of artwork or on a car journey.

Professional and personal boundaries

In practice there are a number of ethical 'grey areas' in relation to working with children. This is often not fully addressed or clear within different organisations, for example, giving birthday cards/presents, buying ice cream or attending an event. Ferguson (2014) discusses giving a child a hug and practitioners' reluctance due to fear of misunderstanding or a potential allegation. Banks (2016) discusses ethics and posits that practitioners should not just be guided by external governance; they should act as active moral agents and challenge rules in relation to social justice and societal compassion. In order to develop authentic relationships with young people there needs to be greater emphasis on blending the personal and professional skills to sustain relationships, for example, appropriate positive role modelling of our own experiences.

Practitioners must learn to use their own professional discretion, accountability and codes of practice, and ethics to stand by the decisions they make in relation to these boundaries. In Northern Ireland these are highlighted within the Northern Ireland Standards of Conduct and Practice for Social Workers (Northern Ireland Social Care Council 2015). There are many social workers who go the 'extra mile' at a personal cost to themselves and not the organisation. Acts of kindness enable relationship-building; therefore they should become integrated and organisationally supported and accepted practice. The *National Occupational Standards* (UKCES 2011) highlight that the social work profession is about problem solving in human relationships. If the profession at its core is about relationships we need to refocus and revise our professional identity and reclaim the very essence of the profession from managerialism as suggested in Chapter 2.

Working with children and young people

Working with children from 0 to 18 years encompasses huge amounts of change and development emotionally and physically. This necessitates practitioners to be skilled and have knowledge of child development theory and methods of practice to underpin good practice. This helps with engaging, communicating and understanding the different stages of how children develop; for example, how we work with infants and teenagers would vary remarkably. When working with young people hormone changes and puberty can impact greatly on behaviour and engagement. Damour (2016) discusses that teenagers may distance themselves from their carers if they are considering risks and decisions that have greater consequences than before. Having knowledge of this behaviour in a social work or care context gives greater understanding of the expectations we have of young people and how we might build relationships.

If we want to engage and communicate effectively with young people we need to continue to pursue different methods, for example, phone, text or through the internet via email, FaceTime or Skype. Young people may find that indirect or non-threatening ways of communication are much easier than direct communication for relationship-building. There is huge value in face to face work; however, practitioners in terms of building relationships need to blend their communication approach with young people. There may be some issues with using social media or other forms of communication; nonetheless, in my experience when building relationships any form of contact, such as a text message, is better than none at all. When applying the Relationship Model in the engagement stage, phone calls and text messages can be very effective.

Relational social work: children and young people

There needs to be more emphasis on spending time with children with a view to building a positive relationship with a child as an intervention in itself, as highlighted in Chapter 1. Winter (2011) would concur that if children have high-quality relationships with their social workers this can enhance their wellbeing and the interventions and services they receive.

There needs to be a blend of skills and knowledge used when trying to establish positive relationships with children using 'soft skills' and age-appropriate communication and blending this with information and advice. Children need consistency of care in order to build trusting relationships. Social workers should be supported by having the resources and skills development to enable these. Social workers need to utilise reflective supervision and critically evaluate the effectiveness of their intervention and skills. There needs to be more skills training with input from young people to ensure there is qualitative feedback from service users to shape the services they receive.

Social work practitioners need to spend time nurturing relationships and these should be given greater emphasis and importance. Often we are trying to repair or establish other relationships in the lives of children and there is too little time spent building one with the child (Winter 2011). Alongside this, practitioners should model and encourage the importance of social capital for 'looked after' children in terms of family, friendships and community. Daly's (2012) research in relation to care leavers highlighted that personal relationships rather than professional ones need to be established along with informal social supports to enable successful transitions from care. Young people need to be encouraged in the value of building and sustaining relationships and giving them a voice in terms of who they identify with and can trust.

Practitioners need to listen to young people and encourage and model positive relationships for them. It can be a challenge trying to build a positive relationship with a young person, for example, when their parents/carers and the people closest to them have let them down or have difficult and conflicted relationships. When children have come into the care system they have received an incredibly powerful message about relationships that for whatever reasons their parent(s) are unable to care for them. This must be a painful message for children to make sense of or process, coupled with trauma. Practitioners need to reflect on this and consider their values, for example, empathy and understanding to really hear and listen to the service user's narrative. This will give us insight, knowledge and understanding which will inform our ability to build effective relationships with children and their families.

When building relationships with children it is important to engage with siblings and wider family members, for example, aunts, cousins, friends or other trusted professionals. Often young people may be reluctant to engage but if you can work with someone close to them and build trust through them this can be very useful. If young people have had lots of contact with professionals and you engage with them after many others they could be 'professionally fatigued'. They have had so much involvement and so many interventions that they have no investment in the relationship and may engage on a very superficial level.

Practitioners when engaging in relationships need to be mindful that there should not be any additional pressure placed on the young person having to retell their narrative unless they want to. Some experiences are painful and often difficult for young people to process until much later on in life. This is why good information-sharing of assessments and reports and multiagency working should minimise any potential stress on initial relationship-building.

Practitioners should never underestimate their impact when working with children and young people. They can work with children for many years and become an important adult in their lives. This has been proved in research in relation to care-experienced young people. In my experience it is not until an ending occurs that the impact may be fully realised. Reflection on endings will be discussed in more depth in Chapter 12.

Young people and leaving care

In Western society young people have become increasingly dependent on their parents from the perspective of a prolonged phase of transition into adulthood. 'The gap between young care leavers and peers with no previous care experiences appears to be widening' (Hojer and Sjoblom 2010, p.125) and this has been evidenced within the current regional, national and international research (Daly 2012; Dixon et al. 2006; Hojer and Sjoblom 2010; Pinkerton 2011; Stein 2008; Ward 2011; Winter 2015).

Young people may be ready to leave care, and those professional and personal relationships that have been established, as well as new ones, may make up the support network. Some young people make the decision for themselves to withdraw from professional support or specifically social work support if they have been dissatisfied with the relationship or had poor care experiences. However, often young people do not want to leave their placement once they reach 18 years old; they may have been in their care placement a long time and considered it as their home (Hojer and Sjoblom 2010, p.123).

Young people may have built extremely positive relationships with either foster or residential carers but because of their age the expectation is that they move on. Gaskell's (2010) and Anghel and Beckett's (2007) research highlights issues with defining an age limit of 18 or 21 and having a 'cut-off point' when young people were forced to leave their placements. Unfortunately this is a poor message when reflecting on relational work that ultimately minimises and undervalues relationships. There needs to be further consideration in the planning process for resources and tailoring packages that meet the needs of individual young adults.

Stein (2008, p.1) advised that 'the journey to adulthood for many young care leavers is shorter, steeper and often more hazardous' than that of their peers. This makes the role of the practitioner critical in terms of having another consistent and reliable relationship to seek support and guidance. There needs to be more emphasis on professional carers and how the relationship is formalised or recognised once young people leave care.

Significant adults and relationships

What has emerged from research is that a 'significant adult' in a young care leaver's life is important in terms of reducing potential risks and aiding a successful transition. Young people need emotional and social support throughout the transition and beyond, thus professional support is not time limited. Gaskell's research identified that 'Many Children in the care system have not experienced a care-giver that they can trust to contain their emotional distress' (Gaskell 2010, p.139).

Daly (2012) identifies social supports as being very important to young care leavers, especially those who do not have family support when making the transition from care. Those personal relationships rather than professional ones need to be established, and informal social supports are very important; this is mirrored in research by Gaskell (2010). However, young people often become isolated and vulnerable and perhaps have few friends or additional supports. Winter (2015) reinforces that one key relationship rather than a multiplicity of relationships can be important and also not to underestimate or minimise the importance of the social work practitioner's and young person's relationship.

Case study: Anne

This is a composite case study which characterises case work with a 'looked after' young person.

Meeting Anne. Anne is 17 years old, white, Catholic, female. Throughout her life Anne has had multiple placements both in foster and residential care. Anne has very little contact with her birth family or younger siblings, who are in foster care placements. Anne has moved to independent living, in supported accommodation in the community. Since moving out into independent living her substance use has increased. Anne has been on a night out drinking and has ended up in the police station for disorderly behaviour. The police contacted both her solicitor and social worker.

Anne was extremely reluctant to re-engage and she was verbally aggressive and called everyone a 'shower of b******s'. This only gave a very small window of opportunity to engage with her in a fairly punitive and negative environment.

The best approach to *engage* was to re-establish the relationship, be caring and offer some company and support rather than the 'professional' lecture about the pitfalls of drinking. The direct and formal approach and risk assessment was not the right way to try and engage. This can be achieved informally through observation. Anne just needed someone to listen, reassure and calm her down. The use of empathy and humour as well as offering solutions to the current situation were appropriate at this time.

Negotiation began when Anne was asked when she left the police station whether she would return to her own accommodation or stay with friends. The preferable answer was to return to the supported accommodation rather than her friends. Experience would have suggested that staying with friends, especially if she had money, usually meant she would go out drinking again. However, it was important that Anne had some choice and control and to talk through the options.

Reflection points

- Given Anne's age it was likely she was going to do exactly what she wanted to do. The suggestion of going back to her accommodation was not popular as she stated, 'I am not returning to that dump.' There was good learning in this as this told me she was unhappy, unsettled and perhaps lonely in her new accommodation and this could be explored at a later date.

- Negotiation skills are crucial when working with young people and trying to be as flexible as possible within the limitations of resources and possibilities.

- Choice is very important when problem solving and making decisions together. Getting Anne to identify the solution was very important and links with values of empowerment.

In order to *enable* Anne she decided to go to her friend's house but agreed I could take her there and collect clean clothes and link in with the supported accommodation first. In the safety planning it was agreed to get a mobile phone and buy credit so if she needed support she could phone.

Anne gave little bits of information about what had happened the night before and rather than challenging her interpretation of the events I listened to her narrative. Anne was aggressive and angry about the police intervention. Anne's perception again gave another insight into her understanding of circumstances and her behaviour. I discussed and modelled appropriately some of my own experiences of socialising as a teenager and what I would do to keep safe, enabling relationship-building and trust.

Reflection points

- Anne is very vulnerable but also acting out 'normal' teenage behaviour, pushing boundaries and challenging, albeit in a more exaggerated or extreme way. Anne is trying to manage complex feelings and emotions.

- In order to enable Anne it was important that she felt part of the decision-making process and part of the solution. With Anne's agreement we arranged to meet again the next day.

- It is important as a practitioner to continue to try and be positive and motivate Anne to take little steps and make good decisions for herself.

Conclusion

Working directly with children and young people requires a huge amount of skills and ability to adapt across the child's developmental range. There has not been the opportunity to consider all age ranges, circumstances or other issues in this chapter. There will be some exploration in Chapter 5 of the model with young people and offending behaviour, and in Chapter 9 with a young person in residential care with the application of the Model of Attachment.

Practitioners need to be creative and seek out opportunities for relational social work but there needs to be change on many levels, politically, organisationally and individually. Practitioners must have the confidence to value the 'unique life histories and narratives' of those with whom they work. They need to avoid routinisation of care planning or barriers to effective engagement and this is explored in Chapter 3. The skill set of the social work role encompasses many facets, such as legal, supervisory and supportive. Building relationships in this complex terrain is not easy; however, using our relational knowledge, skills and values, practitioners need to engage with parents and children as it is fundamental to good childcare practice.

Featherstone, White and Morris (2014) highlight the importance of freeing up time and finance to enable opportunities for building trusting relationships with families and communities. When building relationships with vulnerable young people and their families greater emphasis is needed on encouragement, self-determination and empowerment of service users. Children need their voice to be heard and their views taken seriously in the care planning and review of services they receive. This should not be carried out in a tokenistic way via a 'form' or by participating in very large professionally orientated meetings. The Relationship Model is a simple tool which can be used in practice together with children and young people.

References

Anghel, R. and Beckett, C. (2007) 'Skateboarding behind the EU lorry – the experience of Romanian professionals struggling to cope with transition while assisting care leavers.' *European Journal of Social Work 10*, 1, 3–19.

Banks, S. J. (2016) 'Everyday ethics in professional life: social work as ethics work.' *Ethics and Social Welfare 10*, 1, 35–52.

Curtis, L., Moriarty, J. and Netten, A. (2009) 'The expected working life of a social worker.' *British Journal of Social Work 40*, 5, 1628–1643.

Daly, F. (2012) What do young people need when they leave care? Views of care-leavers and aftercare workers in north Dublin.' *Childcare in Practice 18*, 4, 309–324.

Damour, L. (2016) *Untangled: Guiding Teenage Girls through the Seven Transitions into Adulthood.* London: Atlantic Books.

Dixon, J., Wade, J., Byford, S., Weatherly, H. and Lee, J. (2006) *Young People Leaving Care: A Study of Costs and Outcomes.* York: University of York.

Featherstone, B., White, S. and Morris, K. (2014) *Re-Imagining Child Protection: Towards Humane Social Work with Families.* Bristol: Policy Press.

Ferguson, H. (2014) *Towards Intimate Child Protection: Embracing Children and Keeping Them Safe.* Presentation. The Association of Children's Welfare Agencies (ACWA) Conference, Sydney, 20 August 2014.

Galek, K., Flannelly, K. J., Greene, P. B. and Kudler, T. (2011) 'Burnout, secondary traumatic stress, and social support.' *Pastoral Psychology 60*, 633–639.

Gaskell, C. (2010) '"If the social worker had called at least it would show they cared". Young care leaver's perspectives on the importance of care.' *Children and Society 24*, 136–147.

Hojer, I. and Sjoblom, Y. (2010) 'Young people leaving care in Sweden.' *Child and Family Social Work 15*, 1, 118–127.

Koprowska, J. (2010) *Communication and Interpersonal Skills in Social Work,* (3rd edn.) Exeter: Learning Matters.

Local Safeguarding Children Board Haringey (2009) *Serious Case Review: Baby Peter (Executive Summary).* Available at www.haringeylscb.org/sites/haringeylscb/files/executive_summary_peter_final.pdf, accessed on 4 November 2016.

McCarthy, T. (2015) *A Common-Sense Guide to Improving the Safeguarding of Children.* London: Jessica Kingsley Publishing.

McFadden, P., Campbell, A. and Taylor, B. (2014) 'Resilience and burnout in child protection social work: individual and organisational themes from a systematic literature review.' *British Journal of Social Work 45*, 5, 1546–1563.

Munro, E. (2011) *The Munro Review of Child Protection: Final Report: A Child-Centred System.* London: Stationery Office.

UKCES (UK Commission for Employment and Skills) (2011) *National Occupational Standards for Social Work.* London: UKCES. Available at www.ccwales.org.uk/qualifications-and-nos-finder/n/social-work, accessed on 4 November 2016.

Northern Ireland Social Care Council (2015) *Standards of Conduct and Practice for Social Workers.* Available at http://niscc.info/storage/resources/web_optimised_91740_niscc_standards_of_conduct_and_practice_bluepurple.pdf, accessed on 4 November 2016.

Pinkerton, J. (2011) 'Constructing a global understanding of the social ecology of leaving out of home care.' *Children and Youth Services Review 33*, 2412–2416.

Rogers, M. (2013) *Daniel Pelka Serious Case Review, Coventry LSCB, Overview Report.* Available at http://www.lgiu.org.uk/wp-content/uploads/2013/10/Daniel-Pelka-Serious-Case-Review-Coventry-LSCB.pdf, accessed on 4 November 2016.

Stein, M. (2008) 'Resilience and young people leaving care.' *Childcare in Practice 14*, 1, 35–44.

Thompson, N. and Thompson, S. (2008) *The Critically Reflective Practitioner.* Basingstoke: Palgrave Macmillan.

Turbett, C. (2014) *Doing Radical Social Work.* Basingstoke: Palgrave Macmillan.

Ward, H. (2011) 'Continuities and discontinuities: issues concerning the establishment of persistent sense of self amongst care leavers.' *Children & Youth Services Review 33*, 2512–2518.

Winter, K. (2011) *Building Relationships and Communicating with Young Children: A Practical Guide for Social Workers.* Oxford: Routledge.

Winter, K. (2015) *Supporting Positive Relationships for Children and Young People Who Have Experience of Care.* Insights: Evidence Summaries to Support Social Services in Scotland; No. 28. Glasgow: Institute for Research and Innovation in Social Services.

Wonnacott, J. (2012) *Mastering Social Work Supervision.* London: Jessica Kingsley Publishers.

Chapter 5

MENTORING YOUNG OFFENDERS IN THE REPUBLIC OF IRELAND

Mary Henihan and Julia Alexander

Caring, supportive and consistent relationships have a positive impact on the educational attainment, physical and mental health of young people as well as their general wellbeing (Happer, McCreadie and Aldgate 2006; Siebelt, Morrison and Cruickshank 2008).

There is a growing body of evidence that reveals that one positive relationship with an adult has more beneficial outcomes for young people than multiple relationships (Singer, Cosner Berzin and Hokanson 2013). This is further supported by a large-scale youth mental health study in Ireland carried out in 2012 by Dooley and Fitzgerald. Over 70 per cent of the young people interviewed could identify and valued having 'one good adult' in their lives who they could talk with and share their problems; furthermore, they regarded this relationship as having a positive impact on their mental health, and the research also showed that young people who could not identify 'one good adult' in their lives had more behavioural issues and greater levels of stress and suicidal ideation.

This chapter will discuss two parts of the 4 Stage Relationship Model and focus largely on the engagement stage. It will share with practitioners the importance of investing time in building relationships with young people, the challenges which may be encountered during the engagement stage and examples of what helps to overcome these difficulties. Taking a wider view will enable readers to see benefits of the Relationship Model for both practitioners and young people alike. The chapter will draw on examples and case studies from Le Chéile, a community-based youth justice charity in the Republic of Ireland.

Le Chéile Mentoring and Youth Justice Support Services[1] volunteer-based mentoring model offers young people a unique opportunity to form a relationship with an adult who is not a paid professional. The volunteers give their time each week to mentor a young person and focus on their individual needs and goals.

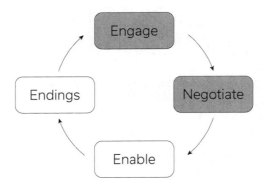

Overview

Le Chéile is a national children's charity established in 2005 to fulfil the Children's Act 2001, Mentor (and Family Support) Order, Part 9, section 131, which is a community sanction. Le Chéile is an Irish term that means 'together' and reflects the organisation's collaborative approach. Le Chéile works in partnership with, and is funded by, the Probation Service to effect positive change in the lives of young people who offend by providing mentoring, family support and restorative justice services.

The current mentoring service emerged from a pilot service established in North Dublin in 2005. The aim of the pilot was to provide one-to-one mentoring services for children between the ages of 12 and 18 who were involved with the Probation Service. Le Chéile uses a community-based mentoring model that utilises volunteers from the community to mentor young people referred by their probation officer. The service is managed by a mentor coordinator[2] whose role is to oversee cases, recruit, train and support volunteers for Le Chéile;

---

1   From here on Le Chéile Mentoring & Youth Justice Support Services will be referred to as Le Chéile.

2   From here on, the mentor coordinator will be referred to as coordinator, volunteers known as mentors whilst young people will be referred to as mentees.

mentoring involves young people meeting the same volunteer each week for up to three hours in their local community. During the first three months all work is focused on building the relationship between the mentee and mentor through activity-based sessions that do not rely on the setting of formal goals. This allows the mentee and mentor to get to know each other without the pressure of achieving targets. All out-of-pocket expenses are met by Le Chéile. After the relationship-building stage, the coordinator meets with the mentee and mentor to review progress, relying on a validated outcome-based measurement tool[3] to assist the mentee to identify areas of their lives where they want to make changes. The coordinator uses the tool regularly with each mentee to help set and monitor realistic and achievable goals. The mentoring sessions gradually become more focused on achieving goals and the mentor supports the mentee with these. The goals vary, from setting up a routine meeting with their mentor on a weekly basis, engaging in positive community activities, such as local sports clubs, through to applying and securing a place in college or finding employment. A mentoring relationship can last between six months and two years. The coordinators review cases regularly with both the mentee and their mentor. The review provides an opportunity to check in to see how the mentoring relationship is developing along with reviewing goals set using the outcome tool.

The young people referred to Le Chéile's mentoring service have all been processed through the court system and charged with at least one offence and are normally on a probation bond (Children's Act 2001). The characteristics of the young people are generally male, with an average age of 17, the majority are still living at home with a parent/guardian and not engaged in mainstream education (Le Chéile 2015–2018). Their offences primarily comprise public order, theft and criminal damage (Irish Youth Justice Service 2013). Many of the young people referred to Le Chéile present with low educational attainment, poor literacy skills, limited maturity, no male adult role model, bereavement and loss issues, mental health issues, negative peer influences and drug and alcohol misuse. Furthermore, many of the young people referred come from minority groups, for example the travelling community, which may have had negative experiences

---

3   *Outcomes Star*™ (n.d.) Brighton: Triangle Consulting Social Enterprise. Available at www.outcomesstar.org.uk, accessed on 8 November 2016.

engaging with agencies in the past. In addition, their parents/guardians can be struggling with their own issues such as health concerns, drug/alcohol issues and housing or financial difficulties. As a result, it can be challenging for the coordinators to convince young people to engage with an adult mentor.

Within the restorative practice framework, the Le Chéile mentoring model encourages mentees' prosocial behaviour, positive behavioural change and participatory decision-making. This is essential in the engagement stage and throughout the mentoring relationship. Restorative practices involve all parties coming together to focus on participatory learning, gaining a greater capacity for understanding, decision-making and putting things right (Watchel 2013; Zehr 2002). In the context of mentoring and the Relationship Model, mentors are encouraged to work with young people throughout the mentoring relationship. This allows for effective relationship-building; it encourages both parties to work together towards certain agreed goals. Throughout this process, mentoring provides the necessary support and encouragement whilst ensuring appropriate levels of control are in place. Furthermore the experience of relationship-building in mentoring will hopefully empower young people's participation when working with social work practitioners and other professionals involved in their lives.

Volunteer model

The unique aspect of Le Chéile's mentoring model is using volunteers to deliver mentoring services. There are several reasons for this, but a key factor is the recognition that many young people already have an array of professionals involved in their lives, many of whom they have poor relationships with (Winter 2015). Mentors provide mentees with an opportunity to engage with and build a positive relationship with an adult outside of their family who is not a paid professional. Le Chéile mentors come from all backgrounds, gender and ages and bring a mix of life experience, skills and qualities to the organisation. It is important to coordinators (and young people) to have a wide array of mentors to choose from when deciding who would be best suited to mentor each mentee. Whilst there is no requirement for mentors to have any particular training or expertise in the area of social care or youth work, applicants have to go through a rigorous recruitment, selection and training process before being offered a position as a volunteer mentor. Qualities such as empathy, patience, understanding and a genuine interest in supporting young people are all key assets. In addition, a warm and friendly personality and excellent communication skills are sought in applicants. Le Chéile believes these qualities and skills are essential in helping to engage, build and maintain a relationship with often hard-to-reach mentees, especially as many of the young people referred for mentoring have not had positive relationships with family members or professionals and are therefore often reluctant to engage with a mentor. Mentors report that it is often the case during the engagement stage that mentees may not turn up for sessions and can exhibit challenging behaviour when they do. This can continue for a prolonged period with some young people who find it difficult to build trust with adults and are wary of engaging with an adult. For this reason, mentors must have the qualities and skills to engage and build a sustainable relationship with mentees and help them regain trust in adults who are involved in their life. Maintaining professional boundaries is a key topic in the comprehensive volunteer induction training that all mentors receive prior to starting as a mentor. In addition, mentors receive ongoing training and regular support and supervision from the coordinator.

Engaging young people

All young people referred to Le Chéile are involuntary clients of the Probation Service but, in order for mentoring to work for the young person, they need to voluntarily engage in the service and see the benefits for themselves. Young people's motivation for engagement at the beginning may vary. They may see the benefits of having a positive role model in their lives and having support at a difficult time in their life. On the other hand, they may merely feel it is expected by their probation officer and the courts. This can impact on the engagement process, as the young person may not be honest about their reason for participating and their motivation could be to avoid a custodial sentence. This can present ethical dilemmas for both mentors and young people. Mentors are not paid professionals, yet the information they report back to the coordinators about a young person's involvement in mentoring can be used in the reports probation officers present in court. In practice this could mean that young people may be selective in what they choose to discuss or disclose to their mentor, if they are concerned about what they will pass on. In either circumstance, Le Chéile staff and mentors are trained and equipped to engage young people who have low motivation to partake in mentoring. One approach which has proved successful is simply to encourage young people to try it for six weeks after which, if they do not like it, they can choose to stop. We find that offering young people a choice and empowering them to make a decision can positively affect engagement. Enabling young people to make their own choices and decisions is similarly important in the negotiation stage of relationship-building. It is also essential from the outset that coordinators explain what is involved in mentoring, so the young person is clear what the role of the mentor is and what to expect from the mentoring relationship. As highlighted in Chapter 1, it helps to clarify expectations and aid understanding at the engagement stage. During the first six weeks, the young people typically start to build a relationship with their mentor and enjoy doing the activities that they themselves have chosen. As a result, the majority of young people not only agree to try the mentoring but continue beyond the six weeks.

The Le Chéile model explicitly recognises the importance of relationships and of allowing time for these to develop, and this in itself is a positive outcome and protective factor for mentees. The focus of the first few months of mentoring is solely about the young person and the mentor getting to know each other and beginning to build a relationship. During this time, no goals are worked on although ideas for goals may be discussed or identified.

A key factor that we believe assists young people to engage in mentoring is that the focus and direction of the mentoring is led by them. For example, the day and time they wish to meet their mentor, what they do during sessions and mentoring goals are chosen, wherever possible, by the young person. In our experience, a young person choosing where to meet their mentor in the community is crucial (particularly in the engagement stage) because they usually pick somewhere they are familiar with and comfortable going to. This can be helpful, for instance, for young people with literacy difficulties who may prefer their local café as they already know what is on the menu. Others feel uncomfortable in what they consider a 'fancy' restaurant or going to a place where they might run into friends who may not know they are involved in mentoring. In our experience, giving young people the opportunity to make decisions about the mentoring sessions and working with them can positively influence the mentoring relationships, particularly at the early stages.

Another factor we believe is key to supporting engagement and relationship-building is the one-year commitment that volunteers are asked to make. This policy aims to reduce the frustration young people have reported in the past of starting to build a relationship with someone who then moves on after a few months. It is well documented that repeated changes of practitioners involved in a young person's life, particularly for those in the care system, can have a negative impact on them (Winters 2015). Moreover, Jean Rhodes (2005, cited in Dolan and Brady 2012, p.85) states, 'Young people who have been damaged by relationships in their lives may find it harder to form an attachment with their mentor.' In recognition of this, Le Chéile does not accept referrals from probation officers to mentor young people for less than a six-month period as there is insufficient time to build a meaningful relationship and work on identified goals. Other factors that have found to be effective when engaging young people is the 'never give up' ethos of the organisation. Le Chéile does not just give young people one or two chances to engage: they persist with efforts to involve them and actively pursue them. Also, we have found involving the young people's family (in Le Chéile, this could mean offering the parent their own mentor) and regularly reviewing the mentoring relationship to celebrate progress when goals have been achieved contribute to a young person's engagement and ongoing involvement with mentoring.

Building and maintaining a good relationship between the mentor and young person is not without its challenges, especially when it comes to reporting safeguarding concerns. However, almost all mentoring relationships survive this if there is a strong relationship in place and if the young person understands that reporting concerns or safeguarding issues are part of the mentor's role and the type of information that has to be reported. On rare occasions, young people forget this or feel that what they have disclosed to the mentor does not warrant being reported. Unfortunately, this can result in the relationship breaking down. This can be difficult not just for the young person but also for mentors. However, it is unusual for the relationship not to get back on track after a disclosure. We believe this is largely down to the young people realising the mentor has a duty to report, the trust they have built up with the mentor and understanding that the mentor is reporting out of genuine concern. With reference to the Relationship Model, it may mean going back to the first stage of engaging and gradually rebuilding the relationship, clarifying roles and boundaries, and the mentor seeking guidance and support from their coordinator.

Application of the model

In our experience and through close consultation with young people and the referral agents, mentoring is deemed a very valuable service. Young people value the fact that the mentors are not paid to spend time with them; they are there because they want to be there.

> Young person: 'The best thing about mentoring is that I got to meet Paula [mentor]. I love meeting her and look forward to it every week.'

> Probation officer: 'It's the potential to develop a very different relationship with the young person. A Le Chéile mentor does not focus on the negative behaviours of the young person and this can be a "breath of fresh air" for the young person.' (Le Chéile 2015)

To further this point we will now demonstrate the young person's level of engagement in mentoring and link this to the Relationship Model in the following case study.

Case study

This case study is a composite of different service users the authors have worked with based on their professional experience. It does not represent any particular individual but the issues presented have been cited in a multitude of cases referred to Le Chéile. This case study will showcase the Relationship Model and particularly focuses on the engagement phase.

Meet John

John is a 15-year-old male. He lives at home with his mother and four siblings. John and his family live in a socially disadvantaged area, with high levels of unemployment, antisocial behaviour and crime. John's mother developed a mental health problem (depression) and she was unable to care for her children and started to drink heavily. John's father had a history of alcohol abuse and was involved with the authorities. From the age of six John exhibited learning difficulties in school but, due to insufficient resources in the school, his issues were not identified; as a result, he now has very poor literacy and comprehension skills. John is a sociable young person and at an early age showed an interest in sport, particularly rugby and soccer, and his father supported his interest. His father left the family home when John was 12 years old and this had a major impact on his life. His behaviour changed and he started to stay home from school and was out late most nights with friends. He gradually started to come to the attention of the authorities for a number of minor incidents of antisocial behaviour. He also started hanging around with a new group of friends that were known to the authorities and he started smoking cannabis. When he did attend school, he was engaging in conflicts with other students and teachers. Things took a turn for the worse for John when he was arrested one night after being caught in a stolen car as a passenger. He was charged and assigned a probation officer, who assessed him and referred him to Le Chéile for mentoring.

Relationship Model in practice in mentoring: from the young person's perspective

On referral to Le Chéile, the coordinator arranges an initial meeting with John to assess the type of mentor that would work best for him and what other supports he requires. The coordinator explores with John what type of a person he would like to be matched with. John was initially resistant to engaging with a mentor. The coordinator fully explained what mentoring involves and that it is voluntary. He further explained that it is a support during his time on probation and a space for him to develop new interests or build on existing ones. The coordinator leaves the information with John and allows him time and space to reflect. After the initial meeting, the coordinator also reflects on the information received. The coordinator determined and reflected on the following:

- John feels alone and he has very little support from friends and family; he presented very low mood and was often sad and this could make it difficult for John to trust and engage with a mentor.

- John's parents are not communicating with him or with each other. Consider how will this impact on the relational engagement process.

- John feels responsible to help out at home and feels he does not have the time to meet a mentor. Is this a barrier to engagement?

- This is John's first time being involved with the justice system. He does not know what is involved, and he is frightened about the thought of going to prison. John also feels that if he does not engage with mentoring, his probation officer will recommend a custodial sentence. How will this impact on his motivation to engage? There is no evidence that there is a supportive adult in John's life at present.

The coordinator needed to reflect on all these points prior to matching John with a mentor. Careful thought and consideration goes into each match to ensure that the mentor can meet the specific needs of the young person. A high level of preparatory work and reflection is essential prior to embarking on the engagement stage.

Failure to do this could prove detrimental to the success of the mentoring relationship. In order to determine what is going on for John, the coordinator uses a person-centred approach and Stage 1 of the Relationship Model. The coordinator uses a soft skilled approach to start the building blocks to the relationship and set the foundation for matching John with a suitable mentor. At this stage, the coordinator must use effective communication skills and active listening skills to engage John. Time is also a useful tool, leaving all information with John to allow him time to process the information provided, and to see if he will engage with mentoring.

The coordinator determines that a positive male role model would be a support to John at this time in his life: a person who has an interest in sports similar to John and someone who is patient, understanding and supportive around his extra responsibilities at home as well as possibly supporting him to improve his school attendance. Finally, the mentor may be required to support him around building a new peer support network and breaking away from his current peers who are having a negative influence on this life.

A few days later John, through encouragement from his probation officer and the coordinator, agreed to a match meeting with his mentor. From the outset, the coordinator anticipated that this would be a difficult case to match, as John was very resistant to engaging with a mentor. The probation officer and coordinator were fully aware of the issues pertaining to John's case. Each person involved had an awareness of the challenges and anticipated potential challenges and blocks. The challenges identified in this case are as follows:

- John only agreed to be mentored to avoid a custodial sentence.

- John does not have time to meet the mentor due to family commitments.

- John does not trust adults after his father left the family home.

- John is afraid to be fully open as he does not want to bring additional attention on the family.

Meet Frank

Frank was one of a group of newly trained mentors recruited by Le Chéile. Frank, a male aged 40, works as a builder and has a keen interest in sport. Frank is gentle in nature and demonstrated excellent active listening stills during the training. The coordinator, after careful consideration, selected Frank to be John's mentor.

The coordinator checked Frank's availability to meet with John weekly and if he would be willing to travel to meet him in the city. This mentoring match was predicted to last between 12 and 24 months. Contact between John and Frank would not continue beyond the 24 months and the coordinator would monitor the relationship closely throughout this period. Frank was given very limited information about John at the time of their match meeting (the first meeting between mentor and young person), but he was aware of certain personal issues that had affected his life to date. At the meeting John established an immediate rapport with Frank. Frank took the lead in the initial conversation, carrying out introductions and asking questions such as 'Do you like sport?' and 'Who is your favourite team?', and using humour throughout the conversation. John was aware that Frank was a volunteer and solely there for him. This made John feel special as Frank was there to help and support him and he was not there because he had to be there. This immediately put the young person at ease. Frank then explained his role fully and they both agreed the boundaries of their relationship and when and where to meet for their mentoring sessions. John continued to meet his mentor weekly and they focused the sessions on John having a space to talk about what might be worrying him at home and supporting him on returning to education. Throughout this process, John developed skills in relationship-building through his engagement with his mentor. John engaged with his mentor for two years. This time was essential to his personal development and to him staying out of trouble. John played an active role in the mentoring relationship; as a result, he is now currently studying for his leaving certificate and has not come to the attention of the authorities.

Unknown to John, Frank was apprehensive going to the match meeting. He was nervous and concerned whether the young person would connect with him, and what if he did not want to meet with him for a second mentoring session?

The coordinator met with Frank prior to the match meeting and discussed any concerns he might have, reminding him of his training and that he would be supported throughout the whole process.

Relationship Model in practice in mentoring: from the mentor's perspective

In order to overcome the identified challenges the mentor adopted a non-intrusive person-centred approach. The mentor allowed time for them to talk and combined it with an activity to put the young person at ease, for example, playing snooker followed by going for something to eat. The relationship phase was slow as John lacked the ability to trust his mentor fully but he was willing to try. He also continued to engage in further criminal behaviour and he was associating with known criminal youths in the area.

The mentor had certain apprehensions, similar to those of any professional when engaging with a new client for the first time. What worked well for the mentor in this case was being non-judgemental, supportive, open, persistent and accepting of John. He provided John with a space to talk, and plenty of time. He was patient and available when John was ready to talk about deeper issues.

The coordinator supported the mentor throughout, by reassuring the mentor that he had the skills and qualities to carry out this role and that he would make a real difference in a young person's life. Even though the mentor was apprehensive of the match meeting, he hid this from the young person and trusted the coordinator's professional judgement and ability to make the right match. The mentor was very dedicated to his role and he had committed the time to volunteer with Le Chéile. He had a genuine interest in working with and supporting this young person.

Receiving proper support and supervision from a trained professional is essential for volunteers/professionals in the field of social work and social care. The coordinator in this case provided both group and individual supervision to Frank throughout.

Reflection points

This composite case study demonstrates mentoring as an example of relationship-based practices, in particular the engagement stage. Throughout this stage the coordinator and mentor both demonstrated soft skills that enabled the mentee to engage effectively with the service and set the initial building blocks to a strong working relationship. It is important for professionals to be clear about their role, set boundaries and agree a contract of work, as well as to empower the young person to engage at their own pace. Knowing and understanding one's own core values is key. The values demonstrated throughout included honesty, empowerment, non-judgement and respect.

Toolkit

This toolkit was devised by the authors to promote effective engagement with young people in line with the Le Chéile mentoring model.

Communicate effectively

Use active listening skills when meeting with the young person. Demonstrate good communication skills such as paraphrasing and reframing so that the young person is clear that you understand them correctly. It is also a useful tool for making the young person feel valued and listened to.

Environment

Provide a safe place for them to talk and share their thoughts and ideas. Work collaboratively with the young person and pick a neutral venue to meet. Ensure that it is accessible and suitable for the meeting and, above all, that the young person feels comfortable and safe to talk.

Role clarity and expectations

Ensure that the young person understands what your role is; be explicit with them as to why you are meeting with them and the purpose of the meetings. State the length of the sessions and how frequently you will meet them.

Agree the parameters of the mentoring relationship and outline what happens when there is a breach of policy, what happens if the young person is in harm's way and what happens if the young person or the mentor/worker is unable to attend a session.

Restorative approach

- Use a restorative practices approach and work *with* the young person. Ensure you provide appropriate levels of support, encouragement and nurture, combined with clear boundaries (Costello, Wachtel and Wachtel 2009).

- Go at the young person's pace.

- Focus on where the young person is at 'in the present' and work at their pace.

- Being patient and persistent is the key.

- Be mindful of any mental health or addiction issues, or learning difficulties, pertaining to the young person.

This chapter demonstrates how the Le Chéile mentoring model works alongside the Relationship-Based Model. In our experience as practitioners we have seen first hand how effective community-based volunteers can be. We have personally found this very rewarding, witnessing young people building positive sustainable relationships with their mentors which empowers the young people to reach their full potential. Furthermore, it is encouraging to see young people recognise the significance of having positive role models, which is important to their overall wellbeing and development.

References

Costello, B., Wachtel, J. and Wachtel, T. (2009) *The Restorative Practices Handbook.* Bethlehem, PA: International Institute for Restorative Practices.

Dolan, P. and Brady, B. (2012) *A Guide to Youth Mentoring: Providing Effective Social Support.* London: Jessica Kingsley Publishers.

Dooley, B. A. and Fitzgerald A. (2012) *My World Survey: National Study of Youth Mental Health in Ireland.* Dublin: Headstrong and UCD School of Psychology.

Happer, H., McCreadie, J. and Aldgate, J. (2006) *Celebrating Success: What Helps Looked After Children Succeed?* Edinburgh: Social Work Inspection Agency.

Irish Youth Justice Service (2013) *Tackling Youth Crime: Youth Justice Action Plan 2014–2018.* Dublin: Government Publications. Available at www.iyjs.ie/en/IYJS/Tackling_Youth_Crime_-_Youth_Justice_Action_Plan_FINAL.pdf/Files/Tackling_Youth_Crime_-_Youth_Justice_Action_Plan_FINAL.pdf, accessed on 8 November 2016.

Le Chéile (2015–2018) *Inspiring Change' Transforming Lives.* Available at www.lecheile.ie/wp-content/uploads/2015/05/Le-Cheile-Strategy-Report-2015_web.pdf, accessed on 8 November 2016.

Siebelt, L., Morrison, E. and Cruickshank, C. A. (2008) *Caring about Success: Young People's Stories.* Edinburgh: Who Cares? Scotland.

Singer, E. R., Cosner Berzin, S. and Hokanson, K. (2013) 'Voices of former foster youth: supportive relationships in the transition to adulthood.' *Children and Youth Services Review 35,* 2110–2117.

Wachtel, T. (2013) 'Defining restorative.' International Institute for Restorative Practices. Available at www.iirp.edu/pdf/Defining-Restorative.pdf, accessed on 8 November 2016.

Winter, K. (2015) 'Supporting positive relationships for children and young people who have experience of care.' *IRISS Insights,* 28. Available at www.iriss.org.uk/resources/supporting-positive-relationships-children-and-young-people-who-have-experience-care, accessed on 8 November 2016.

Zehr, H. (2002) *The Little Book of Restorative Justice.* Intercourse, PA: Good Books.

Chapter 6

RELATIONSHIP-BASED PRACTICE: WORKING WITH OLDER PEOPLE

E. James Todd

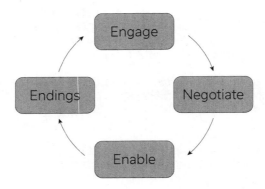

This chapter will discuss the importance of relational practice with older adults and using a real case example to apply all four stages of the Relationship Model.

The working relationship between the social worker and the older person is a dynamic process that can give rise to ethical and practical challenges unique to the client group and the stage of life during which the work takes place. These issues can also be made even more complex by virtue of the expectations portrayed by society, the media and the local political landscape. In the Northern Ireland context the political backdrop includes the challenge of providing care in the community, within the ethos of the 'Transforming Your Care' (DHSSPS 2011) initiative while meeting these demands within an ever-decreasing financial provision by the state. Globally this is being evidenced by increasing demand on health care systems due to non-communicable diseases where the older population accounts for up to 87 per cent of these needs (Dobriansky, Suzman and Hodes 2007). It is anticipated that this pressure will affect not only the statutory provision of the state but also the personal expenditure, and therefore longer-term financial planning, of individuals (Mukherji *et al.* 2015).

It can be somewhat difficult to define who an older (or elder) person is due to a range of factors which include chronological age as well as societal norms (Gorman 2000). Within the Northern Ireland context there is no default retirement age although the state will provide a pension to people over a specified age, generally over the age of 67. However, the legislation establishing a Commissioner for Older People in Northern Ireland interprets the phrase 'older person' to mean anyone who is 60 years of age or older. This is the same age-related definition used by the World Health Organization (WHO 2015) in their report on ageing and health when discussing the ageing population of the world.

While this is an arbitrary definition it is important to remember that the concept of 'elderly' changes across continents, throughout populations, within subgroups and across history. For example the life expectancy of Irish Travellers has been reported to be 15 years lower than the general Irish population (Abdalla *et al.* 2013) with the consequence that a 50-year-old male Traveller might be viewed as elderly within his community but not by wider society. It is, therefore, important when applying the Relationship Model that care is taken to understand the life stage in which the individual feels they belong.

Erikson (1965) has long been cited as a reference guide to what he described as the eight stages of life. When thinking about older adults, he described the eighth stage (age 65–death) as one where there is an internal battle between integrity and despair. However, the picture is becoming more complex than he originally indicated due to increasing longevity in many countries: a fact that Erikson (1998) considered, in collaboration with his wife, in the development of a description of a ninth life stage, which seems to align with the concept of 'real seniors' discussed by Walker (2015). Nonetheless, ascertaining the age at which one moves from being part of 'the young old' (Neugarten 1974) to a real senior appears to be very subjective, with older adults being more likely to report that they perceive themselves to be younger than their chronological age if their academic achievement was higher as a young adult (Shmerlina 2015).

The speech by Jaques to Duke Senior in *As You Like It*, by William Shakespeare, points to the writer having a despairing view of old age. Using the French word for 'without' he describes the last stage of life as 'sans teeth, sans eyes, sans taste, sans everything' (Act II, Sc 7: 139–143). This literary and social history may continue to influence how individuals view the ageing process as a negative one of sequential losses, leading to stigmatising influences becoming internalised and potentially limiting what older adults believe is possible within their unique circumstances. Robbins (2015) reported that the American general public's perception of growing old was a negative one where ageing equates to decline, older adults are viewed as separate from mainstream society and that older people are somehow responsible for their own lack of physical and financial wellbeing. However, she also challenges these perspectives and points to a more positive understanding held by 'experts' working with older people.

This understanding is supported by three interdependent aspects of knowledge, described briefly by Almeida (2010, p.86) as theoretical, practical and ethical dimensions where 'their interlinking influences professional attitudes and performance'. When these aspects come together as a perfect storm then the outcome is more positive for service users and carers, supporting the worker to understand the unique situation occupied by any individual. In a broad review of what older people thought of social workers it is notable they 'prized the skills and qualities of social workers whom they considered were knowledgeable about specialist services, persistent, committed, reliable and accessible, supportive, sympathetic and prepared to listen' (Manthorpe *et al.* 2008, p.1142). All of which points to the value of engaging in a relationship-based approach to social work practice with older people, utilising the 4 Stage Relationship Model.

Engaging

The engagement process normally begins when the worker is allocated a referral which contains the reason for the service request, the contact details of the service user and the contact details of the referrer. The details of the referral letter can carry a hidden message to the reader about the opinion of the referrer. This was sometimes the case with referrals I was required to examine and then allocate for further assessment to a social worker. On some occasions the not-so-hidden message was that the referrer had already concluded a specific service was required and that the social worker was the gateway to accessing the service. While the task of 'gatekeeping' can be a social work responsibility (Dominelli 2009, pp.10–11) it is important to remember that the fundamental tasks of an adaptable and responsive social work practice are much broader and influenced by national as well as agency expectations (Moriarty, Baginsky and Manthorpe 2015).

I can recall a number of such referrals and one which stands out for me was a referral (regarding Mr A) where the 'not-so-hidden' messages were that he had declined medical treatment and that the input of a social worker should result in a change of mind by the service user. It was my perception that the referring health professional wanted a social worker to use their 'counselling' skills to ensure that surgical intervention, for an otherwise life-ending facial tumour, became the client's chosen option.

While the ethics of such an approach are clearly problematic for any social worker it was nevertheless appropriate to ensure that an effective social work service was offered. In doing so the allocated student social worker prepared for the engagement phase of the work by identifying four relationships that could be central to her role in this situation:

- the service user

- the service user's partner

- the referring health professional

- the social worker's professional supervisor.

This phase of tuning-in (adapted from Taylor and Devine 1993) enabled the student to reflect, in professional supervision, on the fundamental values of the social work role – specifically naming ideals such as acceptance, non-judgemental attitude and client self-determination; all of these were described by Biestik (1957), one of the first to write about relationship-based practice.

It is also important to consider that there can be a widely held view that older people are 'willing' rather than 'reluctant' service users. Maintaining this view can delude the worker into believing that engaging in a truly collaborative working relationship will therefore be somehow easier. For many people the introduction of a practitioner into their lives happens at times which can be 'characterised by loss, complexity, multiple needs, change and transition' (Milne *et al.* 2014, p.17). Consequently, the worker needs to be mindful of the fact that their presence can be viewed as a physical manifestation of potentially cumulative losses already experienced by the service user. 'Involuntary clients are often deeply mistrustful of social services' (Smith *et al.* 2012, p.1469). One reason that older people may be reluctant to engage with the social worker is the fact that research indicates older people tend to have decisions about moving into a permanent care facility made for them (Dwyer 2005) and not *with* them. In an attempt to overcome this potential resistance the social work students that I have worked with over the last few years have frequently stated their preference for using an exchange model of assessment (Smale *et al.* 1993; Smale, Tuson and Statham 2000), where each 'partner' in the process can be viewed as holding a level of expertise of benefit to the assessment. This viewpoint enabled the student, working with Mr A, to articulate clearly her own values regarding service user self-determination as a starting point to the assessment of Mr A's needs and how he wanted them met. In turn Mr A also stated to me later that he felt his own expertise, regarding his choice to refrain from medical interventions over the course of his life, was recognised and validated by the student.

Initial contacts can be difficult to prepare for and there is a skill in balancing the unpredictability of these early interactions with the desire to 'get the job done' in an efficient manner. The conclusions drawn by Sullivan (2009, p.1321) indicated that generally social work practitioners and social care workers explained that 'their interactions with older people in the community were managed encounters…to secure an outcome that was right for the community care system and what s/he determined to be a good outcome'.

Relationship-based practice with older people requires the worker to engage in meaningful relationships with a number of people but primarily the older person/service user. The impression that the service user develops of the worker can have a strong influence on whether or not the remaining phases of the model progress effectively. Heckman Coats and Blanchard-Fields (2013) postulate that impression forming has three central components: cognitive, motivational and knowledge-based mechanisms that are interlinked in the development and maintenance of relationships for older people. What is the service user's mental capacity to engage with you? What might motivate (or demotivate) them to engage with you? And what knowledge (perceived or factual) do they hold about you and the role of a social worker? There are questions that you may wish to consider at this stage.

In the early stages of her work with Mr A the social worker carefully paid attention to his life story, identified an area of interest to him and then briefly researched this so that she could ask him some meaningful questions about it. This led to the practitioner and service user recognising each other's sense of humour and personal qualities and supported the development of trust and mutual respect.

Reflection points

Having something in common to talk about with a service user strengthens the relationship-based approach. The difficulty can be that due to generational, sociological or gender differences it may be initially difficult to identify a common area of interest. Try to ask questions about what the other person likes to do, read or watch and use that information as the basis of some research for you.

Negotiation

Agreeing a way forward can be rewarding both for the service user and the social worker as it provides the opportunity to write down the agreed goals and share these with others. On many occasions these goals are developed at hospital-based care planning meetings (CPMs) where group work dynamics, power imbalances and other forces can reduce the active 'participation of the service user. To the point where the older person's participation in CPMs [are] actively facilitated but at the same time ignored, blocked or denied' (Donnelly *et al.* 2013, p.132). In an effort to overcome these problems the use of an integrated assessment tool could be beneficial. Taylor (2012) noted that the collaborative approach taken in the development of the Northern Ireland Single Assessment Tool (NISAT) meant that service users and carers were involved in the design of the framework, stating that this was 'hopefully for the ultimate benefit of older people and their families' (Taylor 2012, p.1308). Using this framework in a variety of practice settings I have been able to see how it has contributed to the service user's voice being more clearly articulated in care planning and assisting other professionals to have a more socially modelled understanding of the service user's needs, circumstances and choices.

This was particularly evident when the option of an 'advance directive' became a central component of Mr A's care plan: to enable him to record and share his 'advance decision to refuse treatment'. There has been a generalised increase in the number of people making advanced decisions across the world (Jeong, McMillan and Higgins 2012; Wee, Weng and Huat 2011), although there are differences between social strata (Carr 2012) and ethnic origin (Carr 2011) regarding the extent of end-of-life planning. In the Northern Ireland context a valid advance decision is not legally binding but would normally be followed by medical staff under common law principles. It is limited to decisions about medical treatment which may be required at a time in the future when the patient has lost their mental capacity to consent, although the person must have the mental capacity to draw up their advance decisions, making clear what treatment is to be refused (or stopped) and under what specific circumstances these actions are to be taken (or not). The exact mechanism for making these decisions, recording and sharing them varies within the United Kingdom, depending on the local legislative arrangements available in England and Wales, Scotland and Northern Ireland. The legal differences between countries within the United Kingdom can be confusing for staff as well as families and it was important that the student social worker, working with Mr A, made effective use of professional supervision to support her own learning and access appropriate resources.

Mr A's expectations of what could be achieved using such an advance directive were beyond what was in truth available to him. The discussions around the actions to be taken (or not) in specific circumstances actually helped him to clarify a more detailed action plan than was his original intention. In many ways the process of agreeing the level of detail (that was required to make the advance directive a valid document) was a negotiation, a process which included the health professional who made the original referral, the ambulance service and Mr A's primary carer.

When agreeing the way forward it can be tempting to solely pay attention to a person's 'lower-level' rather than 'higher-level' needs, using Maslow's Hierarchy of Needs (Maslow 1943), where the lower-level needs focus on access to food, personal care and the completion of practical tasks associated with daily living. This temptation can be reinforced by a health care system built on a model designed to ensure that 'every individual will have the opportunity to make decisions that help maintain good health and wellbeing' (DHSSPS 2011). However, Ivtzan *et al.* (2013) reinforce the view that there is a correlation between age and the higher-level need of self-actualisation, where older people are more likely to evidence self-actualising behaviours than younger adults. Indeed they go on to conclude that, rather than focusing on 'the redundancies and loneliness facing many in old age, we should be looking to these individuals for their insightfulness' (p.129). Looking to Mr A for his insightfulness into his own circumstances enabled the student social worker to understand how Mr A's decision, to decline specific treatment, was in keeping with his life story. It may also have helped Mr A to justify his life (Feil 1985) as he worked towards resolution approaching the end of his life. Additionally, it helped others to understand what treatments would be in keeping with his life story and support him empathetically, effectively and in a dignified manner.

Enabling change

There is a quote from ancient history – 'Change alone is unchanging' (Heraclitus of Ephesus, 500 BCE) – which reiterates the view that nothing stays the same. When life experiences and events 'happen' they influence our life journey and have been described as causing *less conscious* or *more conscious emergent change* by Reeler (2007). Although he was discussing this in terms of community development it nevertheless continues to be applicable in social work practice as *more conscious emergent change* requires supportive conditions which include 'identity, relationships, structures...[and where] the environment [is] relatively stable and less contradictory' (Reeler 2007, p.10). This would indicate that support structures need to be available to respond effectively to the *emergent* needs of the service user and to minimise the disruption to the environment in which the person lives. Similarly, it has long been recognised that the likelihood of successful, lasting *intentional* change is promoted by the availability of a helping relationship or support system (Prochaska and DiClemente 1983).

The support systems available to older people can include family, friends, social contacts and statutory services. It is interesting that, when researching change management, Butterfield and colleagues (2010) reported that 80 per cent of respondents found the support of family and friends was helpful during change and 76 per cent found that their own attitude was an important helping feature. If this data were translated across into the social care sector it highlights the need for social workers to work on two key aspects to enable change to progress: first, to ensure that the family carers are supported in their role and, second, that steps are taken to understand the service user's personal attitude towards the change as the cycle progresses, or repeats.

This was crucial when working with Mr A as many of the supports that developed were designed to enhance his comfort but also to support Mrs A as she prepared herself for her husband's death. On a practical level Mr A had concerns around the fact that his tumour could bleed, as indicated by the consulting physician, so he devised a coping mechanism to support himself and his partner, should this occur. On further investigation by the student social worker it was ascertained that this was not going to be effective. She then in consultation with Mr A took a drawing of his original design to some local tailors and garment repair shops, one of which was able to design and produce a prototype that would apply enough pressure to ensure that the dressing would be effective.

This innovative approach had a threefold effect. It reaffirmed to Mr A that his ideas about how to manage his condition were valid and achievable; this seemed to enable him to also be more accepting of medical interventions that could keep him more comfortable if a major blood vessel erupted in the tumour. Second, it engaged Mr A and his carer in a wider discussion about other environmental and practical preparations that could be put in place – potentially reducing the distress to Mrs A of seeing her husband lose a large amount of blood in the family home. Third, it helped to engage the health professionals involved in a different type of conversation regarding pain relief, use of oxygen within the home and how the emergency services could respond if they were contacted.

Reflection point

The enabling process was enhanced by the level of collaboration that was achieved by effective use of relationship-based practice. The student social worker's practice escalated through the levels of collaboration described by Frey *et al.* (2006), and this shows how enabling change requires the worker to strive towards the point where all the stakeholders have equal authority, thereby achieving a consensus on each of the decisions that needed to be made.

Endings

Achieving a consensus may signal that the ending phase of the working relationship is approaching. However, when working with older people, the consensus is more likely to result in an agreed care plan which requires a statutory review within defined timescales. This is not always the case and, as a practice educator, I have had the privilege of working with students who have been evaluating the ending of their working relationship with older people. In many instances this ending arrives as part of an agreed process and includes the transfer of the key worker role from the student to another professional within the social work team. A planned ending can also denote successful completion of the work with no further intervention required at that stage. However, there are occasions when the ending of the work is preceded by the death of the service user. All endings are unique and it is not always possible to agree how, or when, the work ends, and there can be a sense of grief for the worker in any of the above. This sense of loss is not always recognised by the system within which the work is taking place, which has been described as *disenfranchised grief* by Simpson (2013). This lack of acknowledgement of grief for the worker can be compounded when a 'management style relies heavily on bureaucracy and the completion of associated tasks to the detriment of the necessary cognitive and emotional requirements of social work practitioners' (Simpson 2013, p.86).

The planned ending with Mr A, at the end of the student's practice learning opportunity, afforded the chance for the student to reflect on the emotional impact the work had on her. During supervision she was able to discuss what previous experiences she had of grief and loss and use these to reflect on her current emotion of ending her working relationship with Mr A. While this was a planned ending for her it was very apparent that Mr A's health was also deteriorating rapidly and that his death was approaching, potentially before the end of the student's practice learning opportunity.

Reflection point

On reflection the anticipated death of the service user can be an uncomfortable time for social workers and I have observed how many practitioners described a spectrum of emotions. Feelings of sadness at the imminent, or recent, death of a service user can sit alongside feelings of accomplishment. The worker can feel a sense of professional pride in the role they have played in effectively supporting the individual, the carer and others involved in the journey that was essentially relationship-based practice.

The emotional resilience (Kinman and Grant 2011) and emotional intelligence (Morrison 2007) of social workers become a key strength when 'ending' work with older people. It is essential that social workers take time to consider their own emotional responses to the ending of a relationship as it can help prepare them to engage more effectively with the next phase of relationship-based practice.

The ability to develop and maintain a meaningful working relationship is central to good social work practice with older adults. The fact that the global population is ageing (WHO 2015) indicates that there is an increasing need for social work educators, practitioners and service providers to develop their skills to facilitate working with older adults. The Relationship Model is an effective tool to support practitioners throughout their practice with older adults. Most importantly the practitioner needs to prepare for work by reflecting on why they are there and use their interpersonal skills to 'connect' in a bilateral and congruent working relationship.

References

Abdalla, S., Kelleher, C., Quirke, B. and Daly, L. (2013) 'Social inequalities in health expectancy and the contribution of mortality and morbidity: the case of Irish Travellers.' *Journal of Public Health 4*, 533–540.

Almeida, H. (2010) 'Elderly and social work: values for mediation on contemporary society.' *Socialinis Ugdymas (Social Education) 11*, 22, 84–92.

Biestik, F. P. (1957) *The Casework Relationship.* London: Allen & Unwin.

Butterfield, L. D., Borgen, W. A., Amundson, N. E. and Erlebach, A. C. (2010) 'What helps and hinders workers in managing change.' *Journal of Employment Counseling 47*, 4, 146–157.

Carr, D. (2011) 'Racial differences in end-of-life planning: why don't blacks and Latinos prepare for the inevitable?' *Journal of Death & Dying 63*, 1, 1–20.

Carr, D. (2012) 'The social stratification of older adults' preparations for end-of-life health care.' *Journal of Health and Social Behaviour 53*, 3, 297–312.

DHSSPS (2011) *Transforming Your Care: A Review of Health and Social Care in Northern Ireland.* Belfast: DHSSPS.

Dobriansky, P., Suzman, R. and Hodes, R. (2007) *Why Population Aging Matters: A Global Perspective.* Washington, DC: National Institute on Aging, National Institutes of Health. Available at www.nia.nih.gov/sites/default/files/WPAM.pdf, accessed on 9 November 2016.

Dominelli, L. (2009) *Introducing Social Work.* Cambridge: Polity Press.

Donnelly, S. M., Carter-Anand, J., Cahill, S., Gilligan, R., Mehigan, B. and O'Neill, D. (2013) 'Multiprofessional views on older patients' participation in care planning meetings in a hospital context.' *Practice: Social Work in Action 25*, 2, 121–138.

Dwyer, S. (2005) 'Older people and permanent care: whose decision?' *British Journal of Social Work 35*, 7, 1081–1092.

Erikson, E. H. (1965) *Childhood and Society.* London: Penguin.

Erikson, E. H. (1998) *The Life Cycle Completed: Extended Version.* New York: W. W. Norton.

Feil, N. (1985) 'Resolution: the final life task.' *Journal of Humanistic Psychology 25*, 91–105.

Frey, B. B., Lohmeier, J. H., Lee, S. W. and Tollefson, N. (2006) 'Measuring collaboration among grant partners.' *American Journal of Evaluation 27*, 3, 383–392.

Gorman, M. (2000) 'Development and the Rights of Older People.' In J. Randel, T. German and D. Ewing (eds) *The Ageing and Development Report: Poverty, Independence and the World's Older People.* London: Earthscan.

Heckman Coats, A. and Blanchard-Fields, F. (2013) 'Making judgments about other people: impression formation and attributional processing in older adults.' *International Journal of Ageing and Later Life 8*, 1, 97–110.

Ivtzan, I., Gardner, H. E., Bernard, I., Sekhon, M. and Hart, R. (2013) 'Wellbeing through self-fulfilment: examining developmental aspects of self-actualization.' *Humanistic Psychologist 41*, 2, 119–132.

Jeong, S. Y., McMillan, M. and Higgins, I. (2012) 'Gerotranscendence: the phenomenon of advance care planning.' *Journal of Religion, Spirituality & Aging 24*, 1–2, 146–163.

Kinman, G. and Grant, L. (2011) 'Exploring stress resilience in trainee social workers: the role of emotional and social competencies.' *British Journal of Social Work 41*, 2, 261–275.

Manthorpe, J., Moriarty, J., Rapaport, J., Clough, R. *et al.* (2008) '"There are wonderful social workers but it's a lottery": older people's views about social workers.' *British Journal of Social Work 38*, 6, 1132–1150.

Maslow, A. H. (1943) 'Conflict, frustration, and the theory of threat.' *Journal of Abnormal Social Psychology 38*, 81–86.

Milne, A., Sullivan, M. P., Tanner, D., Richards, S. *et al.* (2014) *Social Work with Older People: A Vision for the Future.* London: TCSW.

Moriarty, J., Baginsky, M. and Manthorpe, J. (2015) *Literature Review of Roles and Issues within the Social Work Profession in England.* London: King's College London Social Care Workforce Research Unit.

Morrison, T. (2007) 'Emotional intelligence, emotion and social work: context, characteristics, complications and contribution.' *British Journal of Social Work 37*, 245–263.

Mukherji, A., Roychoudhury, S., Ghosh, P. and Brown, S. (2015) 'Estimating health demand for an aging population: a flexible and robust Bayesian joint model.' *Journal of Applied Econometrics 31*, 6, 1140–1158. Available at http://onlinelibrary.wiley.com/doi/10.1002/jae.2463/pdf, accessed on 9 November 2016.

Neugarten, B. L. (1974) 'Age groups in American society and the rise of the young old: political consequences of aging.' *Annals of the American Academy of Social and Political Science 415*, 187–198.

Prochaska, J. O. and DiClemente, C. C. (1983) 'Stages and processes of self-change of smoking: toward an integrative model of change.' *Journal of Consulting and Clinical Psychology 51*, 390–395.

Reeler, D. (2007) *A Three-Fold Theory of Social Change and Implications for Practice, Planning, Monitoring and Evaluation.* Cape Town: Community Development Resource Association.

Robbins, L. A. (2015) 'Gauging aging: how does the American public truly perceive older age – and older people.' *Journal of the American Society on Aging 39*, 3, 17–21.

Shmerlina, I. A. (2015) 'Features of the sense of age identity in older age.' *Sociological Research 54*, 3, 203–219.

Simpson, J. E. (2013) 'Grief and loss: a social work perspective.' *Journal of Loss & Trauma 18*, 1, 81–90.

Smale, G. and Tuson, G., with Brehal, N. and Marsh, P. (1993) *Empowerment Assessment, Care Management and the Skilled Worker.* London: National Institute of Social Work.

Smale, G., Tuson, G. and Statham, D. (2000) *Social Work and Social Problems: Working towards Social Inclusion and Social Change.* Basingstoke: Macmillan.

Smith, M., Gallagher, M., Wosu, H., Stewart, J. *et al.* (2012) 'Engaging with involuntary service users in social work: findings from a knowledge exchange project.' *British Journal of Social Work 42*, 1460–1477.

Sullivan, M. (2009) 'Social workers in community care practice: ideologies and interactions with older people.' *British Journal of Social Work 39*, 7, 1306–1325.

Taylor, B. J. (2012) 'Developing an integrated assessment tool for the health and social care of older people.' *British Journal of Social Work 42*, 7, 1293–1314.

Taylor, B. J. and Devine, T. (1993) *Assessing Needs and Planning Care in Social Work.* Alresford: Ashgate.

Walker, B. (2015) 'What does excellent social work with older people look like?' *Guardian*, 14 January. Available at http://www.theguardian.com/social-care-network/2015/jan/14/social-work-older-people, accessed on 9 November 2016.

Wee, N. T., Weng S. C. and Huat, L. L. E. (2011) 'Research note: advance care planning with residents in nursing homes in Singapore.' *Asia Pacific Journal of Social Work Development 21*, 1, 97–104.

WHO (2015) *World Report on Ageing and Health.* New York: World Health Organization.

Chapter 7

BUILDING RELATIONSHIPS TO HELP IMPROVE MENTAL WELLBEING

Stephen Clarke

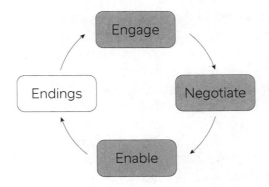

This chapter will begin by considering what mental health is and highlighting the prevalence of mental health problems. A brief review of the biomedical model will be followed by a recommendation of relational work within a recovery ethos, before using a composite case study to illustrate how useful the first three stages of the Relationship Model can be when working with people who have mental health difficulties.

What is mental health?

Whether working directly in a mental health setting or not, social work practitioners will almost invariably, at some stage in their practice, work with individuals who have mental health issues, as the World Mental Health Survey reports that 18–36 percent of the world's population will experience a mental disorder in their lifetime (Kessler *et al.* 2009). Added to this lifetime prevalence rate are individuals whose difficulties may not meet diagnostic criteria, but who are nevertheless in psychological distress and require support. The World Health Organization (WHO 2014) defines mental health as 'a state of well-being in which the individual realizes his or her own abilities, can cope with the normal stresses of life, can work productively, and is able to make a contribution to his or her community'.

Problems that might negatively impact on this definition include common mental health difficulties such as anxiety and depression, and less common problems such as psychosis, where an individual experiences unusual perceptions and loses touch with reality, for example, by hearing and seeing things that others do not (hallucinations). Symptoms can be clustered together in a diagnosis, based on criteria within the *Diagnostic and Statistical Manual* (DSM-5) and the *International Statistical Classification of Diseases* (ICD-10).

However, there is debate about the validity, or even the usefulness, of diagnosing mental distress. Reducing someone's distress to symptoms of a diagnosable mental illness, treatable mainly by medicine, is only one of a number of ways of understanding a person's difficulties when trying to help them. As this book is aimed primarily at non-physicians this chapter will focus on psychosocial factors in relation to mental health problems, particularly relationships. Bentall (2009, p.265) argues that professionals have been blind to the fact that 'distress in human beings is usually caused by unsatisfactory relationships with other human beings'. This chapter will explore how distress may be repaired by using the Relationship Model.

Different views of mental distress
The chemical imbalance view

The biomedical model has viewed mental health difficulties as symptoms of biogenetic illnesses with labels such as depression, bipolar disorder and schizophrenia to name a few. This view, often explained by a chemical imbalance in the brain, has become widely accepted by the general public (Castrén 2005). However, to date, there is no objective biological test that can reliably diagnose mental illness, and the chemical imbalance hypothesis has been criticised due to the lack of robust evidence supporting it (British Psychological Society 2011). One critic, Read (2007), suggests that by minimising the role of social problems the chemical imbalance explanation can prolong a person's suffering by fostering doubts about the benefits of psychosocial interventions. That said, some people find pharmacological interventions helpful, even though the extant literature does not provide strong evidence that medication corrects any underlying biological abnormality.

Stigma

Whilst the biomedical model has been the dominant discourse since the serendipitous discovery of antipsychotic medication in the 1950s (Shen 1999), some believe that it pathologises the individual and is a damaging way to view and respond to a person's experiences (Beresford 2015). For example, if someone is experiencing problems such as prolonged low mood, reduced interest in pleasurable activities, disrupted sleep and eating patterns, difficulty concentrating and feelings of worthlessness, it is plausible to think that a diagnosis of major depressive disorder, explained by an imbalance in serotonin levels, might reduce stigma by promoting sympathy and understanding, as the person is suffering from an illness just like any other. However, Deacon and Baird (2009) found that when participants in their study were presented with the chemical imbalance explanation of a person's problems they were actually more stigmatising, seeing the person as having a serious illness, and being dangerous and unlikely to recover, which may lead to social rejection. On the other hand, when Read and Law (1999) presented participants with information about psychosocial factors contributing to mental distress, there was less stigma.

Diagnosis versus continuum

The biomedical diagnostic categorical way of understanding mental distress (i.e. someone has a mental illness or they do not) – and its assumption that illness is an individual issue, not social – has been challenged by other ways of viewing mental distress. Responding to the American Psychiatric Association's development of the DSM-5 (American Psychiatric Association 2013), the British Psychological

Society recommended that mental distress should be viewed as being on 'a spectrum with "normal" experience and psychosocial factors such as poverty, unemployment and trauma are the most strongly-evidenced causal factors' (2011, p.3). When mental distress is seen as being on a continuum (rather than a categorical diagnosis), and problems are viewed as understandable responses to life's circumstances (including the person's history and present social circumstances), it may be less pathologising of the individual and promote hope that positive change is possible.

Therefore, whilst this chapter considers a case where the service user was given a diagnosis of schizophrenia, practitioners do not need to focus on specific diagnoses to be treated by specific medications or psychotherapies; instead they can use the Relationship Model to build relationships with the person regardless of their diagnosis – that is, person-centred care not disease-centred care, where the relationship might be an intervention in itself, as described in Chapter 1.

Reflection point

As the biomedical model remains the dominant discourse it can be difficult to articulate a different view when working in a multidisciplinary setting. Being mindful of others' expertise, whilst referring to the evidence base, has helped me to ensure that psychosocial factors receive the attention they deserve in care planning. For guidance on relationships within multidisciplinary team (MDT) working, see Chapter 11.

Psychosocial factors

Whilst the chemical imbalance explanation currently lacks conclusive evidence, this does not mean that brain biochemistry is not involved in mental distress, as continued research may further illuminate how biogenetic factors contribute to mental distress. However, within relationship-based practice it is the psychosocial factors involved in mental health problems that are more amenable to relational support. Psychosocial factors that have been found to be contributory factors in mental distress include:

- poverty

- homelessness

- addiction

- abuse (physical/sexual/psychological)

- being part of a minority group (e.g. LGBT community, ethnic minority, religious minority)

- living in a conflict area (e.g. Northern Ireland)

- living in care (see Chapter 9).

Stage 1: Engaging

Many factors can impact on the engagement stage of the model. For example, the relationship may be brief if supporting someone during a short stay in hospital, or it may be longer term in a community setting. If the service user is detained in hospital and treated against their will under mental health legislation, the compulsory nature of this relationship may result in an imbalance of power, and the absence of service user autonomy can make the initial engagement difficult. Michael (see below) was detained in hospital several times, and such experiences can result in a long-lasting fear of engaging with services. The fear of being 'taken away again' can make engagement difficult, and the practitioner needs to consider how such fear, and any other barriers to building relationships, may be reduced.

Composite case study

When 19-year-old Michael moved away to university he became withdrawn, shunned his housemates, became increasingly suspicious of them and began carrying a knife to protect himself. When he started to miss lectures, university staff started asking if he needed support, but Michael withdrew from university and moved back home. He drifted between menial jobs, often being dismissed for poor attendance. One night Michael was picked up by police when a member of the public became concerned about his safety, as he was standing in a distressed state atop a bridge, shouting incomprehensibly at passers by. Whilst detained in hospital under mental health legislation Michael was diagnosed with paranoid schizophrenia and commenced on antipsychotic medication, which he detested (partly as he did not accept the diagnosis, but the side effects were also intolerable for him). I began working with Michael prior to discharge from hospital. Despite two further hospital admissions over a period of three years, Michael managed to move from supported housing to independent living, secure part-time employment, and is considering returning to his studies. Michael's social recovery was matched by a decrease in intensity of his symptoms, although he continues to hear voices on some occasions and sometimes becomes quite paranoid.

Initial engagement

Given Michael's negative experiences of services he understandably did not have much trust in me when we first met, perhaps seeing me as another person within a system seeking to define him as a schizophrenic and control his life, for example, forcing him to comply with treatment. This distrust was gradually overcome by taking a more collaborative approach rather than a directive approach. This is reflected in the Centre for Mental Health's 2012 briefing paper where practitioners were advised to move 'from being "on top" to being "on tap": not defining problems and prescribing treatments, but rather making their expertise and understandings available to those who may find them useful' (Perkins *et al.* 2012, p.2).

Reflection point

Before meeting Michael for the first time I had preconceptions of what he might be like, given his diagnosis of schizophrenia. By reflecting on this prior to our first meeting and wondering how Michael might be feeling having to see me, I reminded myself of the person-centred approach, which enabled me to treat him as I would treat anyone else at a first meeting.

Engagement within a recovery ethos

This collaborative engagement can promote positive change within a recovery ethos, a rights-based framework that has seen the introduction of recovery colleges aiming to empower service users in becoming experts in their own care (Perkins *et al.* 2012). The recovery approach does not necessarily see the elimination of symptoms as the primary goal, but views improved social functioning (e.g. better quality of life, improved interpersonal relationships and engagement with education/employment opportunities) as positive, even if symptoms persist.

Although there is variation in people's experiences of recovery colleges (Newman-Taylor *et al.* 2015) there is evidence of their effectiveness in improving quality of life (Meddings *et al.* 2015a). One area of improvement is the shift in power dynamics. Historically there may have been power imbalances within the practitioner–service user relationship, with the practitioner being perceived as holding power over the service user. However, the introduction of a recovery ethos to mental health services has gone some way to reducing such power imbalances (Meddings *et al.* 2015b).

Yet legislation continues to exist that has discriminated against individuals with mental health problems (Szmuckler and Holloway 2000). Whilst some safeguards are built into mental health legislation, for example, mental health review tribunals in the Mental Health (NI) Order (1986) that applied in Michael's case, mental health legislation is still used to deprive individuals of their liberty. Although the police took Michael to a place of safety (i.e. hospital), he experienced this as authority figures taking him away, and this provoked intense fear in him. This fear was maintained when he began to lose further control over his life when other professionals, who were there to help him, inadvertently added to his distress by labelling him schizophrenic and putting in place a care plan that he had to follow if he wanted to be discharged. Social constructionism suggests that labels such as schizophrenia are social constructs, rather than objective truths, and are part of a mental health pathologising discourse, which puts the balance of power with those who assign the labels, making problems of living more difficult for those living with the label (Carr 1998).

However, labels may not always be unwelcome. Others that I have worked with have been relieved after receiving a diagnosis, finally having a name, and perhaps some kind of explanation, for what has been going on in their lives. Therefore, paying attention to language and power, and working with the service user's preferred understanding of their lived experience, may go some way towards facilitating engagement in the Relationship Model within a recovery ethos.

Practitioner self-disclosure

It may be difficult to view the service user as an equal collaborative partner if the practitioner asks all the questions but reveals nothing about him/herself. Michael once complained, 'That nurse knows everything about me, but I know nothing about him.' The idea of practitioners engaging in self-disclosure with service users carries ethical dilemmas, yet Ruddle and Dilks (2015) found it to be common practice, which may be helpful when working with service users like Michael, who experience extreme paranoia and social isolation. Some potential benefits of self-disclosure include gaining trust at initial engagement; validating a person's narrative by normalising experiences when a practitioner shares universal experiences such as being startled by innocent sudden noises; and explaining that paranoia is on this continuum of experiences (British Psychological Society 2011).

The Scottish Recovery Network (2007) explains that self-disclosure is not always about disclosing facts about yourself, but also revealing your thoughts and intentions. Therefore, explaining what you are thinking and why you are offering particular advice to someone who is paranoid may help reduce paranoia. If a practitioner is to engage in self-disclosure she or he needs to know when it is appropriate, and adhere to boundaries that ensure that any self-disclosure is for the service user's benefit.

Empathy

Tuning into the service user's feelings demonstrates empathy and unconditional positive regard (Rogers 1951), and shows a willingness to understand things from the service user's perspective and to accept and support him or her regardless of what they say or do. Michael did not always believe that practitioners were empathic, and instead of being unconditional their positive regard seemed to be conditional on his behaviour (i.e. adherence to his care plan, which meant taking medication that he did not want to take and attending day care that he hated). As Trevithick (2003) notes, such failure to respond to the service user's real needs generates mistrust, increases anxieties and deepens defences. To avoid this, Stage 2 of the Relationship Model (negotiating) can help practitioners to better understand service users' needs.

Stage 2: Negotiating

The second stage of the Relationship Model (negotiating) can be broken down to substages including, but not limited to, confidentiality, boundaries and goal-setting. Good communication can help avoid misunderstandings and ensure that both parties know what is being agreed at this stage. Although seen as serving a separate function from Stage 1, Stage 2 (negotiating) can often occur alongside engagement, as one of the first items to be discussed with service users is confidentiality and its limitations.

Confidentiality

At the outset, service users must be informed about the possibility that their case might be discussed in supervision, and about confidentiality in relation to record-keeping. Of course, the practitioner cannot guarantee absolute confidentiality and one of the first items to be discussed early in the relationship is the limitation of confidentiality, explaining that if the service user, or anyone else, becomes at risk of harm, then confidence will be broken to safeguard those at risk. Whilst the service user will be made aware of this from the outset, it is when confidence has to be broken that trust can be eroded and a breakdown in the relationship can occur.

For example, after several months of a strong therapeutic relationship Michael started re-experiencing intense paranoia and auditory hallucinations, which resulted in him distrusting everyone. He became withdrawn, and when neighbours became concerned about his unusual behaviour, which was putting him and others at risk of serious harm, I had to advise him that I needed to pass on my serious concerns about his safety. This difficult decision was only taken after trying various other ways to safeguard his safety first, for example employing skills from the ASIST programme (Applied Suicide Intervention Skills Training). Michael's subsequent detention in an in-patient setting affected his trust in our relationship, which required a return to re-engagement (Stage 1) whilst he was still an in-patient, to gradually re-establish trust.

Goal-setting

When trust and rapport have been built (and rebuilt where necessary), goal-setting can begin. Both parties can agree on when, where, and how often they will be in contact with each other, and perhaps at this stage start planning when the relationship will end, in order to avoid abrupt endings at a later stage. For example, in Michael's case it was agreed that he would avail himself of the service until he moved to an apartment of his own, returned to his studies and started repairing relationships with family members.

As described above, collaborative working means that practitioners and service users are equals with equal say in goal-setting. In a recovery ethos people accept support without giving up responsibility. However, some service users may expect the practitioner to be the expert, knowing what needs to be done to 'cure' him or her, and accordingly pass responsibility for change onto the practitioner. It can be a challenge to re-empower people with such an external locus of control to take back responsibility for making changes in their life. When asking for their opinion on goal-setting they may respond with phrases such as 'you know what's best'.

On the other hand, some service users may view goals suggested by the practitioner as further demands being placed on them, and decide to defy someone who they see as having power by disengaging, for example. Practitioners should be open to exploring any items brought to the table by the service user, which can then be negotiated, before moving to achieving these goals through the enabling stage (Stage 3). As each recovery journey is unique, goals will be specific to each service user. Achieving outcomes in goals in these areas may go some way towards realising good mental health as defined by the World Health Organization (2004). Some common areas for goal-setting include:

- issues around discharge from hospital, medication or being re-graded from detained patient status to voluntary patient status

- physical health issues (GP, dentist, smoking, diet, exercise)

- housing issues

- financial issues (debt, budgeting, dealing with welfare claims)

- relationships (with partners, children, peers, wider family circle, employers, etc.)

- training, education, employment

- social life (leisure facilities, gym, clubs, religious and sporting activities, etc.)

- addictions.

The absence of symptoms was not a priority for Michael. When I first met him he was detained in hospital under mental health legislation and his immediate goal was to be discharged. He also wanted support in getting his 'life back on track' which meant getting a place of his own to live and communicating with universities to see if he could restart his studies in a university in Ireland. Other goals included repairing relationships with family, which he believed to be a factor in his symptoms, and he also wanted support in drawing up an advance directive, saying what he would like to happen if he were to become unwell again.

Stage 3: Enabling
Hope and relationship challenges

Having agreed outcome goals, the enabling stage involves supporting service users to achieve positive change. At this stage of the relationship the practitioner may need to provide hope that positive change is possible, as this belief can be absent in people experiencing mental health problems (Scottish Recovery Network 2007). Relationships that promote hope show a belief in the service user's skills, whilst acknowledging that setbacks may occur from which the service user and practitioner can learn (Repper and Perkins 2003). Where setbacks challenge the relationship, practitioners with genuine empathy may notice difficult feelings in the service user and themselves, and they can encourage open discussions about disagreements to help prevent a breakdown in the relationship.

However, if a breakdown occurs, practitioners should acknowledge their own feelings about it. Discussing this in supervision may assist the practitioner to respond empathically and non-defensively with the service user, so that blame is not attributed to either party, and solutions can be found. A practitioner's own negative feelings should not allow him or her to give up on a service user who does not wish to engage following a breakdown in the relationship. Rather, supervision and honest reflection about what happened can help practitioners to try Stages 1 and 2 again.

Attachment and relationships

Exploring and repairing breakdowns in the relationship can help service users experience unconditional positive regard, which may help alter their *internal working models* – mental representations of the self, others and interpersonal relationships, which form the basis of attachment theory (Bowlby 1969, 1973, 1979, 1980). As insecure early attachment is related to adult mental health difficulties (see, for example, Drayton, Birchwood and Trower 1998), and with more securely attached individuals experiencing better outcomes in mental health services (Levy *et al.* 2011), paying attention to attachment style may be useful at this stage.

Being sensitively attuned to the service user and not letting him or her down, for example, by always being there at agreed times, can provide a secure base from which service users can explore the world and try newly learned strategies, in the security of a safe haven to which they can return when needed.

Even when Michael was distrustful, being there consistently for him in the psychiatric ward helped him to gradually re-engage and adapt his internal working model so that he no longer viewed the whole world as an overly threatening place, but could see that there were people who would be there to ensure his safety and support him no matter what his behaviour was – that is, unconditional of positive regard.

To do this (i.e. to be fully there for service users regardless of their behaviour), practitioners need to be confident in their own abilities to engage with individuals whose behaviour may stir up difficult feelings in the practitioner. Fears of working with someone with mental health difficulties, such as a diagnosis of schizophrenia, can lead to prejudice as described above, where the chemical hypothesis was shown to lead to people pathologising the individual and fearing that treatment would not work for them. Such a scenario would make it difficult to instil hope during this enabling stage of the relationship. Where these feelings are not conscious they may become apparent in the practitioner's behaviour. For example, defence mechanisms such as avoidance may manifest in repeatedly missing or rearranging appointments. Therefore, acknowledging one's own defences and prejudices is important as it allows them to be addressed through reflection and supervision.

Organisational pressures

Service models in the current economic climate of austerity place pressure on providers to deliver care under increasingly restricted resources. Links exist between economic policies and mental wellbeing, with increasing inequality between the richest and poorest having long-term detrimental effects (see Marmot 2010). Lack of resources can inhibit relationship-building and may lead to the re-enactment of problematic attachment procedures, such as absence, neglect, invalidation or inconsistency of care. Furthermore, burned-out, compassion-drained staff may find it harder to attune to the attachment needs of the service user (Beck, Mattinson and Sampson 2015). However, co-production may help service users to feel valued within a service user–practitioner relationship.

Co-production and reparative relationships

Co-production requires practitioners to view citizens as equal partners, sharing power to plan and deliver support together, which can promote a sense of purpose and feelings of safety through reparative relationships (Beck *et al.* 2015). Therefore, instead of viewing Michael's auditory hallucinations (voices) as a symptom of a medical illness (schizophrenia) to be medically treated, I took Michael's view of the voices having meaning for him (see the Hearing Voices Movement, www.hearing-voices.org, for more detail on this approach). Michael had been told that he would have to take antipsychotic medication for the rest of his life, but he rejected this idea, as well as the schizophrenia diagnosis. Helping Michael to voice his opinions enabled him to gradually discontinue medication with the help of very supportive medical staff. Validating his experience like this helped to build our relationship so that I was able to help him with the more practical social issues.

For example, Michael was discharged from hospital to a supported housing project for people with mental health problems, but he wanted to move to independent housing. By supporting him to move into his own apartment, Michael began to feel that he was getting his 'life back on track', which was how he summed up the overarching goal at the negotiating stage. Some of his other goals were not completely achieved, but were in progress when I finished working with him. Despite many discussions with universities Michael was unable to transfer to a university closer to home, but he did start a course in his local further education college. He was also well on the way to repairing relationships with family members, and had made an advance directive, saying what he would like to happen if he were to become unwell again.

Conclusion

Whilst prevalence rates of mental health problems are high there is currently no agreement on the exact cause(s). The chemical imbalance hypothesis of mental illness may be flawed, yet many people attest to gaining benefit from pharmacological interventions, whilst incorporating psychosocial factors such as interpersonal relationships, poverty, unemployment and social disadvantage help us understand mental distress within a psychosocial context. This provides opportunities for professional relational interactions to be a source of improved mental wellbeing. The first stage of the Relationship Model (engagement) aims to build rapport with the service user. The second stage (negotiation) leads to agreement on outcome goals which the third stage (enabling) aims to achieve. A recovery approach, with practitioner and service user seen as equals, is recommended.

References

American Psychiatric Association (2013) *Diagnostic and Statistical Manual of Mental Disorders* (5th edn). Washington, DC: Author.

Beck, R., Mattinson, C. and Sampson, M. (2015) 'Co-production in relation to the constructs of mentalisation and recovery in personality disorder and mental health settings.' *Clinical Psychology Forum 268*, 10–15.

Bentall, R. P. (2009) *Doctoring the Mind: Is Our Current Treatment of Mental Illness Really Any Good?* New York: New York University Press.

Beresford, P. (2015) 'From "recovery" to reclaiming madness.' *Clinical Psychology Forum 268*, 16–20.

Bowlby, J. (1969) *Attachment and Loss: Vol 1. Attachment.* New York: Basic Books.

Bowlby, J. (1973) *Attachment and Loss: Vol. 2. Separation: Anxiety and Anger.* New York: Basic Books.

Bowlby, J. (1979) *The Making and Breaking of Affectional Bonds.* London: Tavistock.

Bowlby, J. (1980) *Attachment and Loss: Vol. 3. Loss: Sadness and Depression.* New York: Basic Books.

British Psychological Society (2011) *Response to the American Psychiatric Association: DSM-5 Development.* Leicester: BPS.

Carr, A. (1998) 'Paul White's narrative therapy.' *Contemporary Family Therapy 20,* 4, 485–503.

Castrén, E. (2005) 'Is mood chemistry?' *Nature Reviews Neuroscience 6,* 241–246.

Deacon, B. J. and Baird, G. L. (2009) 'The chemical imbalance explanation of depression: reducing blame at what cost?' *Journal of Social and Clinical Psychology 28,* 4, 415–435.

Drayton, M., Birchwood, M. and Trower, P. (1998) 'Early attachment experience and recovery from psychosis.' *British Journal of Clinical Psychology 37,* 3, 269–284.

Kessler, R. C., Aguilar-Gaxiola, S., Alonso, J., Chatterji, S. *et al.* (2009) 'The global burden of mental disorders: an update from the WHO World Mental Health (WMH) Surveys.' *Epidemiologia e Psichiatria Sociale 18,* 1, 23–33.

Levy, K. N., Ellison, W. D., Scott, L. N. and Bernecker, S. L. (2011) 'Attachment style.' *Journal of Clinical Psychology 67,* 193–203.

Marmot, M. (2010) *Fair Society, Healthy Lives: The Marmot Review.* London: The Marmot Review.

Meddings, S., Campbell, E., Guglietti, S., Lambe, H. *et al.* (2015a) 'From service user to student – the benefits of recovery college.' *Clinical Psychology Forum 268,* 32–37.

Meddings, S., McGregor, J., Waldo, R., Shepherd, G. (2015b) 'Recovery colleges: quality and outcomes.' *Mental Health and Social Inclusion 19,* 4, 212–221.

Newman-Taylor, K., Herbert, L., Woodfine, C. and Shepherd, G. (2015) 'Are we delivering recovery-based mental health care? An example of co-produced service evaluation.' *Clinical Psychology Forum 268,* 50–54.

Perkins, R., Repper, J., Rinaldi, M. and Brown, H. (2012) *Recovery Colleges.* ImROC Briefing Paper. London: Centre for Mental Health.

Read, J. (2007) 'Why promoting biological ideology increases prejudice against people labelled "schizophrenic".' *Australian Psychologist 42,* 118–128.

Read, J. and Law, A. (1999) 'The relationship of causal beliefs and contact with users of mental health services to attitudes to the "mentally ill".' *International Journal of Social Psychiatry 45,* 216–229.

Repper, J. and Perkins, R. (2003) *Social Inclusion and Recovery: A Model for Mental Health Practice.* Edinburgh: Baillière Tindall.

Rogers, C.R. (1951) *Client-Centered Therapy: Its Current Practice, Implications and Theory.* Boston: Houghton Mifflin.

Ruddle, A. and Dilks, S. (2015) 'Opening up to disclosure.' *The Psychologist 28,* 458–461.

Scottish Recovery Network (2007) *Realising Recovery Learning Materials.* Edinburgh: NHS Education for Scotland. Available at www.nes.scot.nhs.uk/media/376420/13875-nes-mental_health-all_modules.pdf, accessed on 8 November 2016.

Shen, W. W. (1999) 'A history of antipsychotic drug development.' *Comprehensive Psychiatry 40,* 6, 407–414.

Szmuckler, G. and Holloway, F. (2000) 'Reform of the Mental Health Act: health or safety?' *British Journal of Psychiatry 177,* 196–200.

Trevithick, P. (2003) 'Effective relationship-based practice: a theoretical exploration.' *Journal of Social Work Practice 17,* 2, 163–176.

World Health Organization (2014) 'Strengthening our response.' Fact sheet. Available at www.who.int/mediacentre/factsheets/fs220/en, accessed on 8 November 2016.

Chapter 8

BUILDING RELATIONSHIPS TO ENABLE CHANGE

A Journey with Service Users and Carers

Uel McIlveen, Geraldine Campbell, Maria Somerville and Brenda Horgan

This chapter examines how the stages of the Relationship Model dovetail with a successful model of building and sustaining relationships with service users and carers[1] in the development of strategy and policy. Specifically, it examines how a regulator of the social care workforce (including social work professionals) ensures that the voice of the consumer, or service user and carer, is at the centre of regulatory activity. As noted by Kirwan and Melaugh (2015), the number of countries where social work practitioners are subject to regulation is on the rise, and therefore service users and carers will have an increasingly important role in helping to shape what regulation of the social work workforce looks like and how it can improve outcomes for service users and carers.

The level and extent of service user and carer involvement amongst regulators differs across jurisdictions. The Northern Ireland Social Care Council (NISCC) model of participation is unique amongst social work regulators in its explicit involvement of service users and carers at the centre of regulation of the social care workforce. Within NISCC, relationships are fundamental – relationships with our staff, our registrants (social care professionals on our register), employers, education providers and, most importantly, relationships with service users and carers who are affected by the decisions which we make. In this chapter we want to explore relationships within the context of the service users and carers

---

1   The term 'service user and carer' is used to describe persons (including recipients or carers) who have been or are in receipt of social work or social care services. It is recognised that in other jurisdictions alternative terms such as 'client', 'consumer' and 'expert by experience' may be used.

with whom we work. Our Model of Participation with Service Users and Carers is loosely informed by the concept of co-production; we aim to illustrate its alignment to the 4 Stage Relationship Model. Within our context, this can be described as 'a meeting of minds coming together to find a shared solution. In practice, it involves people who use services being consulted, included and working together from the start to the end of any project that affects them' (Think Local Act Personal 2011; Social Care Institute of Excellence (SCIE) 2015).

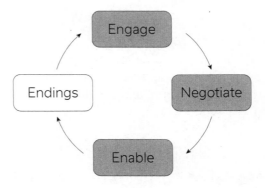

Within this chapter we will focus on the Engage, Negotiate and Enable stages of the Relationship Model. It is unique given that it is the only chapter that has not been written from a professional practitioner perspective. Fundamentally, it examines our participation model and provides reflections from two members of the NISCC Participation Partnership (hereafter described as the Partnership). Members of the Partnership are experts by experience. One member, Uel, is a service user and another member, Maria, is a carer of two children with disabilities. NISCC facilitates service users and carers to have a central role in ensuring that their views, based on their experiences, are reflected in our work. To this end, it is imperative that the right people are involved, that capacity is built and that a meaningful engagement process results in a positive outcome for all. As Uel reflected:

> People join participation groups for different reasons, but people who are genuinely concerned enough to join all have several things in common. Key amongst these is hope: hope that their involvement will in one way or another create necessary change. That hope is vital from the first day, and unless the participant is offered proof that the hope can be fulfilled, they will soon lose interest and effectiveness. Hope is

a basic instinctual emotion that should never be underestimated or undervalued. Hope must also be fed to allow it to grow.

Organisations must acknowledge from the outset that, amongst the many other skills and abilities that participants bring to a group, they possess an expertise that at least matches the expertise of any professional in the room, the expertise of experience. This expertise gives them an equal standing to any professional to discuss the issues that relate to their life experience – their expertise of experience, an expertise that has sometimes had a much higher cost than any university education.

This reflection from Uel emphasises the need for strong foundations to be built to enable a relationship to develop and grow, based on the need of that particular relationship. This point will be discussed more fully later in the chapter, along with the general themes and reflections on the NISCC participation model with respect to the Relationship-Based Model.

NISCC's Model of Participation: overview

Our history of service user and carer engagement dates back to the inception of the organisation in 2001. By 2007 there was a recognition that mere consultation was tokenistic and that we needed to work towards the concept of co-production to ensure an effective service user and carer voice in our decision-making. On reflection, we were at the beginning of a journey of embedding co-production into how the organisation operated, how it defined its values, how individuals worked within the organisation and how we fundamentally made decisions – this is a journey that has not ended.

It was decided that we focus our energies on maximising the opportunity to hear the voice of service users and carers at a level of engagement where they could influence our planning, strategy and policy development. The Partnership was established with the Council, and its remit was, and is, to build relationships with people who have experience of social work/care to enable the Partnership to challenge, influence and advise the work of NISCC. The Partnership, chaired by a non-executive member of the Council, was formally established in December 2008 and is reflected in the NISCC Standing Orders, placing it at the heart of the organisation's governance arrangements.

Engage stage

Our efforts to identify service users and carers who would be able to make a valuable contribution through their skills, knowledge and capacity to learn can be aligned to the Engage stage of the Relationship Model.

In order for the Partnership to work, we needed to build a successful group of the right people. The 'right people' included those who have experience of social care services, those who have the capacity to understand the organisation's role, those who could contribute constructively and those who were willing to listen to others. A person specification and expectations document outlined the skills and experience required and mutual expectations.

We engaged with voluntary sector organisations and service user and carer groups to identify potential service users and carers who met the specification, and who were interested in becoming involved in the work of NISCC. We carried out discussions with each potential member against a set of competencies, a two-way opportunity to learn more about each other. Service user and carer feedback reflected on the shared understanding which this created, as Maria reflects:

> At this point, there was an almost formal recruitment and selection process. Although this was slightly daunting, from my perspective it was important. We were aware of the expectation on us. We were all selected due to our individual skills, competencies and qualities. We were made aware that our membership would be for two years, but this could be extended depending on ongoing pieces of work we were involved in.

This is further reflected by Uel, who summarises the initial engagement process:

> Identifying why people choose to participate is important. Those reasons can give insight to the individual and how best to make use of them. Inviting people to join groups without some in-depth assessment of their suitability can be damaging to the wider group. There is a need to ensure that participants are willing to give as much as they reasonably can to the project, and not just use their involvement as a 'personal kudos badge', not using the title without accepting its responsibilities.

Equally useful is identifying the skills/abilities of individuals. This then means that tasks allocated match skills, giving the most satisfying and productive result for all concerned.

In parallel, we established a set of expectations and a 'contract' with NISCC staff. It was important to ensure that staff were equally as committed to excellent participation, and that they recognised the value of engaging with service users and carers. Warren (2007) emphasises the importance of facilitating participatory practice, and highlights that one of the biggest barriers to the achievement of participatory practice is professionals' inability to distinguish between partnership, consultation and information-sharing. We created the space for staff to discuss and explore what partnership really means.

To build group cohesiveness we organised an intensive two-day workshop facilitated by the vice-chair of the Partnership, who was an experienced group-work facilitator. This 'forming' stage of group development (Tuckman 1965) enabled members to move from orientation and exploration to building trust. Maria and Uel report that it also helped to instil a sense of shared ownership, with everyone as equal stakeholders in the group with an important part to play. This 'investment' in the dynamics of the group acted as a basis of agreeing the way in which the Partnership would work. We continue to do this when there are significant changes within the Partnership, as this is a group of individuals who, unlike staff within an organisation, only come together once every 6–8 weeks. They do not have the usual opportunities, therefore, to build trust, share values, learn about each other and understand the place which that person will have within the team. Uel reflects:

> Not everyone will be a vociferous participant immediately. Some will take a few meetings to find their feet, to establish a clearer understanding, to feel confident to speak. Distinguishing those from the disillusioned can be difficult, but is necessary. Giving time to those who need it, along with some support and encouragement, will pay long-term dividends.

Negotiate stage

When we recruit new members we instil the need for them to challenge, influence and advise the work of NISCC which we revisit at each appraisal meeting. According to Uel and Maria, this expectation has enabled them to understand that their input acts as a definite vehicle to effect change. They understand the purpose and what is expected of them within this framework. Maria reflects:

> The role of the service user and carer Partnership was very clear. My experience working with different agencies is that very often they are unclear about your role with them, and their engagement is ad hoc and haphazard. NISCC was explicit about the role of the forum and its functions within the broader NISCC context. We were very clear about the three functions of the Partnership. As the group has evolved, it has become much more embedded in the structure of NISCC and has become increasingly important to all aspects of the work in NISCC. It was clear from the outset that a lot of planning had taken place before the Partnership had formed.

We are always open about the limitations, either on us as an organisation by external bodies or limitations within the organisation. That is not to say that they cannot still be challenged and we have a 'no secrets' policy with the Partnership. This honesty helps to build trust, and shows that we value and respect the members enough to share the challenges that exist when making decisions.

Maria and Uel advise us that the use of language around defining the parameters of how a relationship will work is very important. For example, the use of the word 'challenge' is very powerful, making them feel that it will be welcome and does not need to be dressed up as something else. They also say that it is crucial to building trust that when challenge is delivered, that it is handled appropriately. They believe that there is a tendency among professionals to become defensive when there is challenge.

Reward is very important. Everyone has to get something from the relationship to want it to continue. None of it is monetary, so as an organisation we have to work to ensure that the reward is sufficient to encourage continued commitment. One member reports that they gets the greatest satisfaction from seeing documents that contain the changed phrasing in them that they suggested – their actual words. That is why they keep coming back: because they knows that they are making a difference as an individual. Another member likes the way in which they have felt part of something bigger and commented that they were treated as an equal, albeit with different roles to play.

The Partnership believes that there is a great need to balance the process of contracting with a level of informality in order to put members at ease. Our meetings are as informal as they can be, as we believe that this brings out the best in service users and carers. Our experience has shown that it is more likely that service users and carers will feel confident enough to be able to contribute effectively in a relaxed atmosphere. We place great emphasis on comprehensive induction which is regularly repeated and essentially never-ending, and is part of the balance in the relationship-building capacity of the individual as a reward for participating. This point is well articulated in Uel's reflections:

> participants must be made to feel valued..., encouraged and inspired by access and feedback... A good friendly collaborative relationship between participants and organisation... working within remit, but not afraid to go "off topic" where necessary or useful, digressing to allow for relationship building banter...

Enable stage

On our journey towards meaningful engagement, in addition to the two areas covered under Engage and Negotiate stages, we recommend that there are two other important elements to this process: there need to be a shared set of underpinning values within an organisation that support best practice in this area, and capacity-building is imperative. Capacity-building needs to be on two levels. First, it needs to develop the skills and knowledge of the individual to contribute efectively and, second, it needs to also build their confidence and self-esteem, and therefore their own personal capacity. The benefits to service users and carers form sucessful involvement are well documented by Warren (2007). Personal benefits relate to increased confidence, self-esteem, self-belief and skill enhancement. The dynamics of group work (collective involvement), as highlighted earlier in the chapter, can bring about personal empowerment and a sense of being heard and listened to. These positive personal outcomes are apparent among our members and correspond to the Enable stage of the Relationship Model. Maria's reflection provides testimony of this:

> This leads me to the enabling role NISCC has had in my life. My experience in NISCC has helped me in my personal circumstances.

I feel valued. I have represented NISCC, giving presentations at various multidisciplinary events and conferences. I have chaired a conference as a representative of NISCC. I have been involved in adjudicating the social work awards and now sit on the ten-year Regional Social Work Strategy steering group. I am co-chair of the Citizens' Forum of the Strategy, having been nominated by NISCC.

For us, enabling is about ensuring meaningful involvement that partly comes from listening to service users and carers about their experiences of what have been barriers in the past to achieving this:

> Don't work for us, work with us! We know what has been beneficial in the past, and what has been frustrating, because of time spent achieving little. At an organisational level, include us in timetabling. Family commitments may mean no availability after school hours or during school holidays; health and medication issues may limit our availability and effectiveness as well. (Maria's reflection)

As part of the enabling process, we have developed 'Principles of Participation', which were first developed by the Partnership and then collectively explored and committed to jointly by staff and the Partnership working together. Primarily, they were designed to set out the parameters of the relationship, collectively commit to what meaningful engagement would look like and to provide a framework within which the NISCC and the Partnership would complement each other to ensure successful outcomes. The six overarching principles – which are supported by commitments under each principle and associated quality standards – are:

- leadership
- partnership
- communication
- supporting involvement
- evaluation
- governance.

The establishment and embedding of the Principles has facilitated a positive working arrangement within NISCC at all levels. This can be illustrated from Maria's reflection when she comments:

We are all too aware of tokenism within organisations. What we need to do is look at the quality of engagement. What has been crucial about the engagement with NISCC is the recognition and value placed on our expertise. I know I have expertise, but I also know that NISCC value and recognise my expertise.

It is important to pay close attention to this enabling role within NISCC. The facilitators of the Partnership are non-social work staff. This is important as service users and carers do not feel threatened as users of social work services; all recognise the power imbalance within the service user and carer social worker relationship. The facilitators are very skilled in communications. They use very enabling language. They support us as a group but importantly as individuals as well. We regularly receive phone calls of encouragement and support when undertaking individual pieces of work within NISCC...

...the Partnership builds and strengthens our capacity...

...has certainly increased my self-esteem and self-confidence. I know that the professionals in NISCC and the members have a sense of belief in me, and know that I will represent NISCC in a positive manner. I do feel genuinely supported and enabled by them.

Language is very important in effective enabling or disabling of an individual. Partnership members tell us that they listen carefully to the language that we use and determine from it whether we will live up to our promises. Uel sums this up well with the following reflection:

Meeting up with each other face to face, planning the agenda, and providing easy read material really helps me. When I am in meetings, the group takes the time to break down the information; they repeat information and speak clearly. This all helps me to feel heard.

Clear unambiguous language is vital. Frequently perceptions are as important as reality; a line used out of context can undo much good work.

Uel cites an example of empowerment through his membership of the Partnership. He reflects on increased confidence and skill enhancement when he delivered his first ever key note speech at a major social work conference that showcased how people with experience of social care could work in partnership with professionals:

I never foresaw myself in that role. At some point, I recognised that being a member of the Partnership had given me the ability to develop a strategic overview of certain issues and the further ability to articulate that position. The next logical step was to express those views personally, but with the Partnership's support.

Both Uel and Maria believe that experiences like those described above are very important because it is a form of validation. As Maria describes, 'This sense of validation is critical to us as service users and carers. Without it we could not continue. It is especially important as our role is a voluntary one.'

A fit-for-purpose set of guiding values or principles should lend itself to eventual effective embedding of meaningful partnership working with service users and carers. This participation of service users and carers in the work of an individual professional should become part of their daily practice, and not be a one-off activity. Members believe that it is not coincidental that there is this ethos of enabling within the Partnership, because NISCC recognises as an organisation that the input of service users and carers is quite often the most powerful input into a piece of work. Staff and Council itself see and recognise the value of co-production in developing better decisions, leading to better outcomes. This is reflected in the following comment from Jan, an NISCC professional adviser (social worker):

> Throughout my employment at NISCC, my work with the Participation Partnership has shown me the value of meaningful involvement with service users and carers. Involvement brings a richness and depth to my work. For me, this is best reflected through their contribution to the annual Northern Ireland social work awards. They have been involved as panel members, selecting finalists and winners. Their contribution has influenced the application pack, the selection process and the running of the entire event. NISCC cannot afford to be without this group and the input of its members.

Part of this initial embedding process can be supported by 'champions' within the organisation until such time as the partnership approach becomes an integral element in the professional's way of working. Members of the Partnership have recognised the importance of such champions within NISCC, as discussed by Maria:

> I feel what has really enabled me and the Participation Partnership is the presence of 'champions' within the organisation. I feel they are deeply committed to hearing the service user and carer voice and they advocate for this throughout the organisation.

The reflections illustrate how the relationship has evolved. It demonstrates belief in members' capabilities and gives them an increasingly wider platform. Uel speaks of the hope that is generated at the Partnership, giving him hope to raise other issues and a belief in a system of Partnership working that can effect true change. Not only does this have a positive effect on the individual and mutual benefits for improved decision-making and outcomes, but it also builds confidence that service users and carers can effect change given the right conditions. Maria and Uel highlight that NISCC has enabled members to use the skills which they were selected for, whilst acknowledging individuals' different capacity, and creating the right environment to enable individuals to flourish. This can be seen, for example, in the development of a previous member of the Partnership, who was appointed to the NISCC Fitness to Practise Committee where she serves as a lay member on committees looking at the fitness to practise of professionals on our register.

There have been many achievements over the previous eight years where members of the Partnership have improved, enhanced, enriched and changed the outcomes of NISCC's work. One great example of this is in the development of the core Standards of Conduct and Practice for the social care workforce in Northern Ireland. Our relationship, based on mutual respect and trust, is at its most powerful when the service user and carer influence the core activities of the organisation, as the following demonstrates:

> The role of the Partnership in shaping the new NISCC Standards of Conduct and Practice (NISCC 2015) has been key. These Standards outline the values, attitudes, behaviours, knowledge and skills required for competent practice. Their involvement in shaping and promoting the Standards has brought home to social care registrants the importance of consistent, value-led practice from a service user and carer perspective. Service user involvement encourages 'buy-in' from registrants, that the Standards have been developed using a bottom-up rather than top-down approach. It's harder to argue against them when they have been shaped by service user and carers' experiences and expectations. (Helen, professional adviser)

Other major pieces of work have included development of the consultation materials and joint delivery, with the lead professional adviser, of seminars to explore the issues around changing from a

Code of Conduct model of regulation to a Fitness to Practise one. Members of the Partnership have developed strong messages aimed at social work professionals and others about how their work impacts on service users and carers on a daily basis through development of communication materials, multimedia products and speaking opportunities at conferences, ministerial visits, etc. and judging social worker awards. They have contributed to the development of post-qualifying education policy and planning for social workers, and have played an important part in the preparation for rolling out registration to non-social-work social care staff.

It is important that opportunity for a review of progress is built in and that this lends itself to ongoing enablement. To this end, we review with staff, through formal appraisal, how involvement has supported their work and what we could do better. With the Partnership members, we pose similar questions at annual feedback sessions, allowing members to assess themselves against key areas such as how they feel they are contributing strategically, what areas they feel they need to develop and what can be improved. As reflected by Uel, this is seen as a beneficial exercise for all members:

> This helps to make everyone aware of who would be the most appropriate person to engage in any piece of work that comes our way, and also reassures members that they are playing to their strengths while being supported to work on areas they may wish to develop.

While recognising the positive messages from Maria and Uel, Maria also refers to the need for NISCC not to become complacent. This reflects the continuum of our Model and how it needs to be reviewed, strengthened and developed with service user and carer engagement. In essence, this process recognises the need for regular opportunities to take stock of a relationship, and recognises that it is imperative to invest in the mechanics of the relationship if it is going to be effective. For example, our future plans include the need to document more clearly the impact of the Partnership working with service users and carers. This process will start with thinking about evaluating impact at the early stages of the design phase of a piece of work or project so that we are clear from the start how we are going to show what has changed as a result of service user and carer involvement.

Our model has been central to the enabling process as identified by McMullin as the following comments show:

As service users and carers, we are used to professionals feeling they know what is best for us. In true partnership working, professionals should adopt an approach of 'What do we need to know and do to best support you?' We want professionals to know what is important *to* us as well as what is important *for* us. I believe NISCC have this approach. It is a much more natural and dignified approach. (Uel)

The manner in which NISCC has engaged with us has determined how effectively we have been enabled as a group and as individuals. This ultimately has been an empowering experience for me. As a carer, I have very often felt 'on the outside looking in' at services. This is a very isolating and disempowering experience. Within NISCC, I have felt 'on the inside looking out', a very different place to be. (Maria)

This chapter has aligned the NISCC Model of Participation of Service Users and Carers to the 4 Stage Relationship Model. It has focused on three stages of the Model – Engage, Enable and Negotiate – and has reflected the views of members of the NISCC Participation Partnership about what has been important at each of these stages to building effective relationships. NISCC have been successful in ensuring meaningful participation to bring about change in the development of social care regulatory policy and strategy. The key components across the three stages outlined include, first, ensuring that our service users have the right blend of skills, knowledge and experience; second, building capacity in the broadest sense – capacity to contribute effectively in terms of understanding the context in which a decision is being made but also building the individual and personal capacity of each member; third, clearly defining roles, remit, responsibilities and expectations; and, last, respecting expertise, skills and difference, and building on these and valuing the contribution of service users and carers as equal partners in the relationship.

We have embarked on a journey of co-production, and as we are focused on continuous improvement we believe that our journey is never-ending. Continuous growth and learning will strengthen the path that we journey. The framework for the Model emphasises the need to take time to build relationships at the engagement stage, and to build capacity to nurture the enabling stage. It illustrates how to build relationships with service users and carers that are mutually beneficial and based on trust, respect and recognition of expertise and validation of experience.

We have facilitated service users and carers to become central to the core activities and work of NISCC – they are now an integral part of how we work and what we do as a result of effective relationship-building. This chapter demonstrates how trust is implicit in this relationship, and to be trusted one needs to trust. This applies to all involved in a relationship. Having established trust, this forms the cornerstone of the relationship, and the stage is set for achieving positive outcomes that can be mutually beneficial and far reaching.

Reflection points

Service users and carers feel enabled when they are valued, respected and listened to, and when they are an equal partner in a process of decision-making. This can have positive ripples throughout their personal lives. How might you bring this concept of enablement into your day-to-day interactions with service users and carers?

Service users refer to the 'power imbalance' between service user and social worker being an impediment to meaningful engagement – how do you, as a practising social worker, address this perceived or actual imbalance?

There are elements within relationship-building which can be reflective of group-work theory, such as 'contracting' and building a sense of a group ready to achieve positive outcomes.

It is important to have a set of guiding principles and values to ensure that everyone is on the 'same page' and is clear what is expected of them in a partnership like this. This form of commitment, kept regularly under review, provides the framework under which any joint working is undertaken. Does your organisation have a shared sense of how meaningful engagement should happen with service users? Have service users been part of the development and review of those values that are used? NISCC Principle and Quality Standards for Participation are available at our website www.niscc.info/participation-partnership.

When considering the 'how to' of co-production, the Social Care Institute of Excellence (2015) recommends a framework for change management, structured around a four-piece jigsaw covering culture, structure, practice and review. For further information on co-production, see Social Care Institute of Excellence (2015).

References

Kirwan, G. and Melaugh, B. (2015) 'Taking care: criticality and reflexivity in the context of social work registration.' *British Journal of Social Work 45*, 3, 1050–1059.

Northern Ireland Social Care Council (NISCC) (2015) *Standards of Conduct and Practice for Social Care Workers and Social Workers.* Belfast: NISCC. Available at http://www.niscc.info/registration-standards/standards-of-conduct-and-practice, accessed 10 November, 2016.

Social Care Institute of Excellence (2015) *Co-Production in Social Care: What It Is and How to Do It.* SCIE Guide 51. London: SCIE. Available at www.scie.org.uk/publications/guides/guide51/index.asp, accessed 9 November, 2016.

Think Local Act Personal (2011) *Making It Real: Marking Progress towards Personalised, Community-Based Support.* London: TLAP.

Tuckman, B. (1965) 'Developmental sequence in small groups.' *Psychological Bulletin 63*, 6, 384–399.

Warren, J. (2007) *Service User and Carer Participation in Social Work.* London: Learning Matters.

Chapter 9

RESIDENTIAL CHILDCARE
Relationships in the Group Care Environment
Lynn Connor, Adrian McKinney and Paul Harvey

Residential childcare is a choice for many young people (Institute of Public Care 2007) and therefore is necessary in the provision of care through government policy and strategic planning. Within the United Kingdom there have been many inquiries and reviews of residential provision based on institutional abuse and bad practice. The continual struggle to improve services and provide better experiences and more positive outcomes is cited in many reports which recognise that residential childcare will always be a needed resource (Audit Scotland 2010; House of Commons Education Committee 2014). It is, however, recognised that good residential childcare has its place, can provide a safe, positive and therapeutic environment and can effect a positive difference in the lives of children (House of Commons Education Committee 2014).

Relationship-based approaches in residential childcare have been developed internationally, for example, the Orinoco Care Program of the Maples Adolescent Treatment Centre in Canada (Leaf 1995), and attachment-informed practice is being prioritised in the delivery of childcare services in Scotland (Furnivall 2011). Macdonald *et al.* (2012) reviewed international research on therapeutic models of residential care in their study of the models being piloted in Northern Ireland at the time – Social Pedagogy, the Sanctuary Model, ARC (Attachment Regulation and Competence), MAP (Model of Attachment Practice) and CARE (Children and Residential Experiences). A common positive thread found across all models was the importance of attachment and relationships. Kendrick, Steckley and McPheat (2011, p.13), in a similar study in Scotland, noted that

'The most dominant themes of relationships and lifespace provide powerful mediums for enhancing development, promoting resilience and providing reparative experiences.'

In this chapter we consider the first stage of the 4 Stage Relationship Model outlined in Chapter 1, asking what we consider when we 'engage' in a relationship-based approach within residential childcare. As a practitioner in residential care there are many relationships to be negotiated – those with children we care for and those with adults we work with, during any one working day. Successfully creating engaging relationships with a child, or with and between the group of resident children and the staff team, can be a tricky process yet is one of the inherent challenges to be met within a residential setting. Within residential childcare in our Health and Social Care Trust we have developed a relationship-based approach called the 'Model of Attachment Practice' (MAP). The theoretical drivers underpinning this model have informed our approach to this chapter.

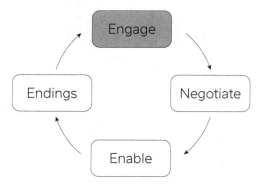

In considering the Relationship Model we were struck by how frequently any relationship within a children's home could cycle through all four stages many times in one day. There are natural cycles of 'connections', 'disconnections' and 'reconnections' that occur within any relationship, but particularly within residential childcare.

The specific challenge to be faced is how to repair the damaged sense of relationships that will have developed for the children living in our children's homes. Many of them will enter residential childcare as teenagers, their relationships at home with their family or foster family having broken down. They will have been hurt, and become frightened and wary of relationships with others, adults in particular.

When new relationships begin to slowly emerge and form they are all too often fragile, unfamiliar and all at once welcome and unwelcome for our young people. The tenacity, the resilience, the creativity, the energy needed by practitioners working within residential care to see beyond the anxiety and rejection of these hurt young people is immense.

Working within residential childcare carries within it a distinct opportunity (or challenge) for those who choose to work there. The very public arena of our children's homes means that to work within residential childcare can bring with it a risk of feeling scrutinised, observed, constantly on duty, on show. Practitioners within residential childcare have to juggle and balance individual needs, wishes and wants (their own and the child's) with the needs, wishes and wants of the group (the team's and the children's) not just for an hour or two, as in other social work settings, but for the duration of the working day (or night).

Lewin (1951) defines this setting as the 'life space'. It is not a space within which it is possible to hide even if you were so inclined. Breakfast, lunch, dinner and tea breaks are all shared with 'service users'; this is not a phenomenon typical within many other settings in professional life. Fewster (1991) outlines a view which is perhaps at the crux of any relationship-based approach, but seems particularly pertinent when we bring our minds to what is needed for those working within residential care. He highlights the significance of our contribution as individuals to our caring role and the influence of this on our behaviour in our professional role.

Relationship-based practice: is it doing or being?

One of the fundamental principles of MAP is that it is a way of 'being' as opposed to a manualised prescribed way of 'doing'. This principle is grounded within our belief that relationships are, and relationship-based practice is, a way of being with each other, all of us who enter under the roofs of our children's homes. We believe that we don't 'do' relationship-based practice: we choose to think about 'how we are' in the relationships we form with others, our colleagues and service users.

Smith, Fulcher and Doran (2013) refer to the challenge of residential social work, those aspects that mark it apart from the other domains of the social work profession. They speak of the roots of residential care in Great Britain, often born from the notion of abandoned or forgotten children who needed to be rescued, educated, managed, moulded, to become valuable members of society – the emphasis being upon their behaviour as something that needed to be eradicated, shaped or controlled so that it would fit and conform to some expected societal norm. This task was not one, particularly in the earliest years, which was viewed as the domain of social work, with many charitable organisations and religious orders taking on the mantle of caring for children at that time.

Just as Smith *et al.* (2013) speak of the forces that were brought to bear upon children in residential care over the years, they also allude to the forces that have buffeted social work as a profession over the decades, and residential social work in particular. They cite the 'professionalisation' of social work as a phenomenon which shifted the focus of the social work task. The inclusion of residential childcare as a domain for the profession was something which came to delineate the focus of the residential social work task. 'Professionalisation saw a shift away from the live-in staff who had been at the heart of previous models of care to what Douglas and Payne (1981) call an "industrial model", in which the personal and professional selves of carers became separated' (Smith *et al.* 2013, p.249).

In many ways to subscribe to a belief that it would be possible to separate the personal and the professional aspects of our 'self' is one which seems within the tenets of relationship-based practice to be entirely erroneous. It sits at odds with Fewster's assertion of the significance of an individual's inherent contribution to the caring task, as something which supersedes their professional role behaviour. Within MAP we place the highest value upon the relationship that exists between ourselves and young people, highlighting that the greatest resource available to any practitioner within residential childcare is their capacity to form relationships with young people.

The roots of relationships

Proponents of attachment theory John Bowlby (1969) and Mary Ainsworth (1973) highlight that from the moment we are born we have a fundamental need to be in a relationship with another. As a tiny dependent newborn our very survival depends upon it; in the weeks, months and years ahead, these primary attachment relationships form the bedrock of our individual development and the foundation from which all other relationships evolve.

Systemic theorists posit that from the very moment of our birth we become part of our first social system, our family of origin. The experiences each of us have within our family group begin to shape and influence the blueprint we develop for relationships, something which Bowlby named our 'internal working model', a mental map for understanding our self, others and the world.

The influence of these earliest attachment relationships and the potency of the family group are critically important to understand when considering our service users. However, we believe that relationship-based practice requires us to develop an understanding of this for ourselves also.

As the practitioner our role can seem clear: we have a task to fulfil, an intervention to complete, an outcome to deliver. Often it can be difficult to find enough time, let alone the time necessary to ponder the commonalities of these beginnings we share with our service users and the influence they carry into our relationships with them. As practitioners we are often ascribed the role and position of expert, as the source of advice, knowledge and support – a seductive role to be given. However, for any practitioner within residential childcare this reflection upon our beginnings is one of the necessary challenges to be faced.

The multiplicity of relationships

Reflective practice has become a mainstay in our children's homes, providing an environment within which we can reflect upon our practice and our relationships within the homes, those we have with each other and those with the children. Together we consider not just what is happening in the 'here and now' (as Gharabaghi (2012) puts it) for the child but also what is happening in the 'here and now' for the adult.

We believe that in any relationship that exists between two individuals there are three relationships rather than one relationship at play. We acknowledge that whilst to the onlooker it might seem that in the 'here and now' they are observing only the one relationship, which exists between the two individuals, the child and the adult, there are in fact three relationships exerting their presence and influencing the dynamic that exists between them. The most evident relationship is the one which exists between the two of them in the here and now, but each individual also has a relationship with their own past – the 'there and then' that each of us has lived, our own history formed from our relationships with significant others in our life – which cannot help but be carried with us into the 'here and now'. As a consequence, in any interaction between us and another person we cannot avoid being influenced by our own history and neither can the person standing across from us.

It seems a reasonable starting point for any of us when attempting to engage in relationships with our clients that we begin by trying to understand them. Within any setting and most certainly within residential childcare it is possible to draw upon an expansive theoretical base pertaining to children and their families. We often turn to theories of child development, attachment, trauma, resilience, social learning theory and many more in our attempts to make sense of the children we are caring for. The difference within our relationship-based approach MAP is that we consider how this theoretical base helps us to understand ourselves, as well as the children and families with whom we work. Reflective practice groups and individual reflective supervision create an environment that enables us to understand our 'there and then' and the influence this has upon our relationships within our work setting with children and with our team colleagues.

We believe that unlocking the potential for engagement in relationships depends not upon the young person, but upon us. Furthermore, unlocking the potential for engagement is not the result of some clever technique or particular line of questioning. The potential for engagement lies in the feeling we create for our young people upon first meeting them and upon every meeting with them thereafter.

It can often be that, when we find our relationship with a young person challenging, we locate the source of the difficulty as residing within them and not upon the experience we are creating for them. Perhaps uncomfortably for us, the challenge is how we can be curious about ourselves first, attempting to understand what we bring to our relationships with others 'warts and all', as the first step to unlocking the possibility of engagement with young people. When we strive to understand ourselves in connection to those we work with we create a different foundation for relationships, a different basis for engagement.

Intersubjectivity

Choosing a career in residential childcare necessitates an acceptance that we are choosing to become part of the 'life space' of children. When we enter into relationships with them, we are entering into a process which has the capacity to influence us and affect us, as much as the children with whom we work. This process of reciprocity is characteristic of any of those relationships in our world which feel best for us. Being present with another will, inevitably, if we allow it, have the power to influence the feelings and the experience of each of us individuals in that relationship. Dan Hughes, consultant clinical psychologist and creator of dyadic developmental psychotherapy, draws his readers to the concept of intersubjectivity and its power within relationships. Hughes (2011) states that, 'Intersubjective communications involve the sharing of experiences where each one is open to both influencing and being influenced by the experience of the other.' Creating intersubjectivity is something which we strive towards in a relationship-based approach.

The concept can perhaps be elucidated with a playful little tale of an experience where sadly intersubjectivity disappears. He describes a couple who have been dating for a while, really enjoying each other's company and getting to know each other as the months have gone by. Sitting across a candlelit table one evening one is heard saying to the other, 'I just want to say how wonderful this all has been. I enjoy being with you so much, I really feel that we have grown so close and could have an amazing future together!' They go on to say (and this is the part where not just the loving feeling but the intersubjectivity disappears) 'I have noticed a few little things about you which I have found increasingly irritating as time has gone on, but I am sure if you could just sort those out we could be so happy together!'

This tale, perhaps rather humorously, illustrates the power of intersubjectivity and the hurt that can be experienced in its absence. This example may seem worlds away from a professional setting, but in many ways it is not. How often do we say to the young people we work with, 'You know what? You've been doing really well recently. The only thing that's really unsettling it all is how you handle yourself when you're angry. There is this really friendly counsellor we could send you to who could work on that with you – what do you think?' A relationship-based approach necessitates challenging ourselves to consider what experience a young person might receive from how we are with them and from what we say to them.

Hughes (2011) really helps us to understand how to make an experience intersubjective, one which feels valuable and useful for both staff and young people. He defines three key aspects (discussed below) involved in ensuring a relationship is intersubjective. When it comes to the task of engagement with our clients, our paying attention to creating something which feels intersubjective communicates our wish to be only with them and nowhere else at that moment. It conveys our wish to try to understand their experiences and their perspectives in that moment, letting go of our pre-planned agenda.

Creating engaging relationships

Hughes (2011) cites 'affect regulation', 'joined awareness' and 'complementary intentions' as being the hallmarks of intersubjectivity. Affect is described as a nonverbal communication, a nonverbal expression of feelings. When we are with someone and interested in only their experience we can't help but notice things about them – their posture, their facial expression, their stillness or lack of it – which give us a sense of how they might be feeling right at that moment. Our own affect then becomes an important aspect of communicating our interest in them, our wish to understand them and the manner by which we can communicate our empathy for them.

'Joined awareness' means that both the client and the professional are paying attention to the same thing. For example, if a young person is upset and angry about another staff member having spoken to them about their drinking and staying out late the night before, and we have the sole focus of trying to get them to understand why our colleagues might have said that, we are focused on the experience of our colleagues, not on the experience for the young person. We are not joined with them in paying attention to just how annoying it was for them to have the staff member talk to them about the night before. In bringing our awareness to how horrible it feels to have staff talk to them about such things we get the opportunity to stay in the moment with the young person and, it is hoped, get the chance to discover more about why it all feels so difficult for them.

Having 'complementary intentions' is about both individuals wanting the same things from the time being spent together; with 'complementary intentions' there is an inherent balance between what we want as practitioners and what the young person wants. So if the children wanted to watch a big football match on Wednesday evening but staff wanted to spend some time having a young people's meeting like they always do at 7.30 pm on a Wednesday, there will be a certain degree of jarring of intentions, and a little flexibility is needed in order to resolve the situation with relationships remaining intact!

Reflection points for creating caring relationships

We have attempted to weave the teachings on intersubjectivity within MAP. We consider the difference between caring for our young people and caring about them; we highlight that a relationship-based approach must have both. We believe that it is possible to 'care for' without creating the feeling that you 'care about'; we challenge ourselves to consider how we might create both for our children in our homes. Very simple things woven into the way of being together in our homes can create the feeling of both. From always making sure the brand of tomato ketchup or flavour of crisps the young people like is in the cupboard, to picking up a magazine for them when you're not working because you noticed the group they like is on the front cover, to spotting something in the local press that they might like to go and see with you – all create a feeling of being 'cared about' as well as 'cared for'.

Creating an environment that engenders a feeling within our children that they might wish to 'engage' with us is the responsibility of us as adults. One of MAP's guiding principles is that 'The emotional atmosphere is the responsibility of the adults!' Often cited alongside this principle is the colloquial phrase for illustrative purposes: 'If you go to work with a face like thunder, you are going to get… lightning!' We are asked to notice how we are when we come to work – what are we bringing with us when we cross the threshold of our children's homes? What feeling will we create for the children who live there?

It's all about PLACE!

Within MAP a fundamental task in engaging with our young people is to connect to and with them, and their experience. Our young people need to feel our wish to get to know them, to understand the world from their perspective – our desire to 'get' how things feel for them and what that might be like. It is a task, but it is not a mechanistic, methodical, prescriptive one. It has fluidity about it, an open-endedness. It's a cumulative process of moments in time spent with a young person and experiences shared together. When we approach our time with our young people with the only goal in our minds being to connect to what their experience is, or has been, a different attitude emerges. Hughes (2011) calls this the attitude of PLACE – playfulness, love, acceptance, curiosity and empathy. It is the attitude which is embedded within dyadic developmental psychotherapy, but it is an attitude which can be found just as easily beyond a therapy room.

One only has to observe those earliest hours and days of a new parent with their healthy newborn to see the joy, the love, the fascination, the curiosity and the wonder with which the parent approaches this newest relationship in their life. Everything is there to be discovered, explored and wondered about: the tiniest fingernails, the length of their toes, whose nose they have, what colour their eyes might be, how they like to be held, how best to get them to sleep. Everything about this newest relationship is accepted, even the most unpleasant parts of it: sleepless nights, early mornings, endless nappies and so on. The communication in this first relationship does not rely on words and language and does not rely on both parties taking responsibility for the success of the relationship. The onus of responsibility resides with the adult, who soon learns that taking time to work out what might be going on for their baby first will lead to a better chance of them being able to adapt their behaviour to meet the needs of their child in that moment.

Composite case study

And so to PLACE within the realm of residential childcare, where Jane, a staff member, notices when she comes on shift that the now familiar strains of 'Avici' are loudly emanating from Eve's room. The team have been really worried about Eve recently and her evasiveness about who she has been spending time with when she is out of the home. The team have all noticed the pattern emerging with Eve: loud music from the moment she wakes up, spending hours getting ready, staying away from staff, refusing breakfast, lunch, offers of doing something else with staff during the day and then leaving the home and not coming back until the small hours, under the influence, argumentative and aggressive. The challenge of engaging Eve in any way has become increasingly difficult.

Jane had been thinking about Eve that morning before leaving home for her sleep-in. She, like her colleagues, has been very concerned about her. She decided to bring her hair straighteners in from home, hoping Eve might allow her to at least spend a little time with her straightening her hair for her before she heads out. On the way to the office as she arrives at work Jane spots some of Eve's clothes in the tumble dryer in the laundry room. She drops her belongings in the office and returns to the laundry, taking the opportunity of folding Eve's clothes and bringing them with her to Eve's room along with the straighteners.

Jane knocks cheerily on the door and when Eve shouts out 'What now? What the **** do you want? I told you, Mike, that I didn't want any breakfast!' Jane gently opens the door and says 'Hey hey hey! It's alright, it's not Mike, it's me. I saw your clothes sitting and I thought there might be something in the pile that you wanted to wear today so I brought them down to you. Plus I know that song is your 'heading out' song and I wanted to see if you wanted a hand with your hair or anything. I brought in my straighteners from home; your hair looked lovely last time you let me straighten your hair with them. Anyway it will give us a wee chance to spend five minutes together before you head out; you know we always put the world to rights when we get a bit of girly time like this!'

Jane had succeeded in getting to spend a little time with Eve before she said to her that she wanted to head out, as Jane knew she would. Even though Jane was worried, she knew she had gently broached the topic in her conversations with Eve, so instead said, 'I'll drop you wherever you want to go, sure. I was going to head out to the shop anyway and get a couple of those Pot Noodle things you like to have when you get in at night. I'm sleeping in tonight and I thought I could get it ready for you when you get back. You know me, I love my wee midnight feasts! I'll take five minutes with you whatever end of my day I can get them. You're my wee star!'

On the drive Eve becomes quieter and intent on texting and responding to the numerous texts that ping on her mobile every couple of seconds. Jane follows Eve's directions, mentally taking note of where she is leaving her, all the while trying to keep the time they are having together as light as she possibly can. Just before Eve goes to jump out of the car Jane says 'Hang on a wee minute. Let me fix that fringe again. There now – you are looking just lovely; just you be sure to keep our wee chat on your mind when you're out there this evening! I'll be thinking about you and you know if you need me to make that Pot Noodle any earlier just you holler and let me know! Be sure to send me a wee text now and let me know you're okay and I will see you when you get in!'

Reflection point

Jane could easily have approached her time with Eve that day very differently. Her anxiety about her could have prompted her to try to have a serious chat with Eve about the dangers that she and the team were all concerned about. She could have insisted on a contract with Eve agreeing a time for her to return and some reward if she did. She would have been able to document all of this in Eve's file and give a comprehensive handover to staff of everything she had told Eve. She would have cared for Eve, but would Eve have felt cared about?

The relationship that Jane had developed with Eve meant that she often crossed her mind when she was at home, especially when anticipating seeing her again as she prepared for each shift. Bringing in her straighteners in the hope of straightening Eve's hair would have demonstrated to Eve just how much she was on Jane's mind. The opportunity for a catch-up the moment she came on shift would give Eve a sense of how important she was to Jane, and the carefully folded laundry would hopefully allow her to feel Jane's wish to look after her and help her in whatever way she could. Jane's shift was peppered with little gestures which she knew Eve would like, which Jane hoped would allow Eve to feel nurtured, respected and valued.

Reflection point

The fact that Eve would be forefront on Jane's mind when she was out that evening and that she was anticipating the opportunity of a midnight Pot Noodle would hopefully allow Eve to feel the connection between them and the warmth of Jane's regard for her. Jane held hope that lots of little moments like these with Eve might some night result in a little text from her telling her to get the kettle on, that she was on her way back for that Pot Noodle! What a moment that would be to celebrate in a relationship-based approach!

Relationships then are something which we strongly believe should be prioritised in our children's homes. We believe they are our responsibility as the adults, successes resting on the atmosphere and the feeling that we create. Organisationally we strive to support our professionals with this approach – with comprehensive training, individual supervision which focuses on relationship-building, and fortnightly team reflective practice sessions. Relationship-based approaches do not replace the many other wonderful and necessary aspects of social work practice, but without the relationship they will certainly struggle to succeed.

References

Ainsworth, M. D. S. (1973) 'Attachment, exploration and separation: illustrated by the behaviour of one year olds in a strange situation.' *Child Development 41*, 49–67.

Audit Scotland (2010) *Getting It Right for Children in Residential Care.* Edinburgh: Audit Scotland.

Bowlby, J. (1969) *Attachment and Loss: Vol 1: Loss.* New York: Basic Books.

Douglas, R. and Payne, C. (1981) 'Alarm bells for the clock-on philosophy.' *Social Work Today 12*, 23, 110–111.

Fewster, G. (1991) 'Editorial: the selfless professional.' *Journal of Child and Youth Care 6*, 4, 69–72.

Furnivall, J. (2011) 'Attachment-informed practice with looked after children and young people.' *IRISS Insights*, 10. Glasgow: IRISS.

Gharabaghi, K. (2012) 'Translating evidence into practice: supporting the school performance of young people living in residential group care in Ontario.' *Children and Youth Services Review 34*, 1130–1134.

House of Commons Education Committee (2014) 'Residential children's homes.' *Sixth Report of Session 2013–14, HC 716*. London: Stationery Office.

Hughes, D. (2011) *Attachment-Focused Family Therapy Workbook.* New York: W.W. Norton.

Institute of Public Care (2007) *What Works in Promoting Good Outcomes for Looked After Children and Young People?* Cardiff: Social Services Improvement Agency.

Kendrick, A., Steckley, L. and McPheat, G. (2011) *Residential Childcare: Learning from International Comparisons.* Glasgow: Scottish Institute for Residential Childcare.

Leaf, S. (1995) 'The journey from control to connection.' *Journal of Child and Youth Care 10*, 1, 15–21.

Lewin, K. (1951) *Field Theory in Social Science: Selected Theoretical Papers,* ed. D. Cartwright. New York: Harper & Row.

Macdonald, G., Millen, S., McCann, M., Roscoe, H. and Ewart-Boyle, S. (2012) *Therapeutic Approaches to Social Work in Residential Childcare Settings.* Belfast: Institute of Childcare Research, QUB, DHSSPS(NI), Social Care Institute for Excellence.

Smith, M., Fulcher, L. and Doran, P. (2013) *Residential Childcare in Practice: Making a Difference.* Bristol: Policy Press.

Chapter 10

THE SUPERVISORY RELATIONSHIP WITHIN PRACTICE LEARNING

Denise MacDermott and Susannah McCall

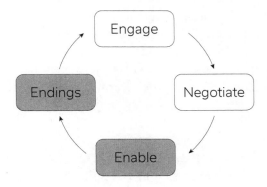

This chapter will examine the application of a Relationship-Based Model of social work in working with students engaged in practice learning opportunities with service users. It will concentrate on the 'engaging' and 'ending' stages of the Relationship-Based Model, examining the dynamics between the practice teacher–student relationship and the student's relationship with the service user. Ford and Jones (1987, p.23) identified the primary function within the practice teacher–student relationship as 'to help the student become aware of the nature of the job to be learned and to acquire the knowledge and skills involved in responding to people's needs in a helpful way'. This definition of the primary function still holds currency. So we know what is required within the relationship but how do we get there? In social work practice there is a range of 'narratives' ever-present in the supervisory relationship. These include the overarching social and political narratives, the practice teacher's narrative, the student's narrative, the service user's narrative, as well as other stakeholders who have a role within the context of the work. The challenge for the practice teacher is to enable the student to begin to reflect critically on their own narratives, alongside the 'unique life histories' of the individuals, families and carers with whom they are working. Within the literature there is a significant body of evidence which supports the role of critical reflection in facilitating transformative learning and development (Baldwin 2004; Fook and Gardener 2007; Taylor 2007). For practice teachers, this requires moving away from didactic approaches by recognising 'what students bring' to practice learning and how students' experiences are validated by encouraging students to view these experiences as a starting point for critical engagement with service users. Brodie and Williams (2013) conducted a small-scale study of supervision using audio recordings of supervision sessions. This offered a rare insight into the relationship between the practice teacher and student. Relationships which were viewed as open and honest and where the student had an active role in identifying and developing their learning were key factors in levels of student satisfaction in terms of the 'quality' of the student–practice teacher relationship.

As a practice teacher and professional social work supervisor, I am interested in the mutual learning that occurs within the supervisory relationship. I view supervision as a reciprocal relationship, whereby helping the student to explain and understand their relationships with service users, listening to their perspectives on the 'how' and 'why' and unpacking the emotions all offer new learning for me. Weld (2012, p.15) concurs: 'what the supervisee brings from their experience creates the potential for growth and change for the supervisor'. Occupying an interchangeable role as both teacher and learner has enabled me to reflect on my own narratives, my self-awareness and self-knowledge, and contributed to minimising the inherent power dynamics within the supervisory relationship.

This chapter will explore the practice teacher–student supervisory relationship and, using two interlocking narratives, will look at the dynamics occurring between the practice teacher–student relationship and the student–service user relationship. The authors will draw on the Relationship-Based Model as a critical reflection tool in supervision. Within all of this is the importance of dialogue to create and sustain understanding between the practice teacher and the student and from the student to the service user. The construction of new personal meaning through critical reflection and discourse is what Mezirow (1990, p.1) describes as the 'heart' of adult learning: 'the process of making a new or revised interpretation of the meaning of an experience, which guides subsequent understanding, appreciation and action'.

The practice learning context

One of the key aspects of practice-based learning is that students learn as a result of the experience (Kolb 1984) Within the social work profession, practice-based learning is recognised internationally as the signature pedagogy (Bogo 2015; Boitel and Fromm 2014; MacDermott and Campbell 2015; Wayne, Bogo and Raskin 2010). Practice learning opportunity (PLO) is the term used in the UK to describe the professional practice component of the degree in social work, with practice teachers being the term designated to qualified practitioners who are responsible for assessing the student whilst on placement. In Northern Ireland this requires completion of a specific post-qualifying taught course at master's level. International colleagues will be more familiar with the terms field practicum/field education and practice educator. However, for the purposes of this chapter the authors will use the term practice teacher.

Within practice-based learning all social work students are required to evidence their competence and demonstrate acquired skills, knowledge and values to intervene across a range of practice settings, including working with individuals, families, carers, groups and communities. At the heart of this are relationships and the students' ability to develop and demonstrate 'relational competence' in working with service users. Practice teachers are positioned as 'ideal' role models, who can emphasise the value of self-awareness, by sharing their own practice experiences with students including the challenges they experienced.

In assessing students' professional competence against the required Standards for Practice Learning for the Degree in Social Work (Northern Ireland Social Care Council (NISCC) 2009), the practice teacher has a professional responsibility to ensure that the student is 'fit to practise' as a social work practitioner. 'Practice learning is therefore a core element of professional training that prepares social work students for entry into the profession' (NISCC 2009, p.1). The role of assessment can present anxiety for both the student and the practice teacher. From the student's perspective, there is a clear power imbalance within the supervisory relationship and students may sometimes feel vulnerable. The practice teacher holds the keys as 'gatekeeper' to the profession – in this role, they have more authority and more practice knowledge. To this end, the supervisory relationship between practice teacher and student is a central tenet of the student's experience of practice learning.

For the practice teacher, this gatekeeping role is critical, as service users require protection against poor/incompetent practitioners. The 'Service User Movement' is much more involved in the design and development of social work education and describing what they think a 'good social worker' should have as part of their professional toolkit. Moreover, the governing body for social work in Northern Ireland, in their 'Readiness to Practise' report (NISCC 2013), identified increased service user and carer involvement as a key element of professional social work training.

Role of the practice teacher

Handy (1999, p.60) comments, 'Any individual, in any situation, occupies a role in relation to other people. Her performance in that role will depend on two sets of influences: the forces in herself – her personality, attributes, skills and the forces in the situation.' The role of the practice teacher is complex. The practice teacher is responsible for helping students to become professional practitioners and to develop the knowledge, skills and values associated with their professional role and identity. Scholar et al. (2014, p.1001) summarise the definition of professional identity as 'the attitudes, values, knowledge, beliefs and skills that are shared within a professional group, and related to the professional role being undertaken by the individual'.

The experienced practice teacher has a range of knowledge gathered over their many years of practice experience. Boitel and Fromm (2014) divide this into three types of knowledge: tacit, reflective and procedural. There are also practitioners who are new to the role. They have to manage the 'dual roles' of practice teacher and student, as they too are assessed on their competence to 'pass' and qualify as a practice teacher. The challenge for both seasoned and 'new' practice teachers, however, remains the same: to help the student to reframe and observe relationships and interactions between people. This is the challenge as supervision is an interactional and intersubjective process and whether aware of it or not, both the student and the practice teacher are sending relational cues to one another about their relationship.

In my own experience as a practice teacher, I have worked with a wide range of students across settings including adult services, children and families and youth offending. The significance of the practice teacher's role to facilitate students to 'internalise' both implicit and explicit knowledge should not be underestimated. From my own experience, understanding the interplay that exists between tacit and explicit knowledge in building relationships is key to enable learning and exploration in developing social work students' competence. To achieve this students need a positive learning environment and time to build relationships. This requires returning to our roots in social work, highlighting the power of past relationships and experiences (Urdang 2010). Students who could identify the different narratives between themselves and others, and who could see the 'bigger picture', interpret and acknowledge the emotional responses involved, were able to demonstrate their 'relational competence'.

A key element of being an effective practice teacher includes understanding how adults learn best. In my own practice I value Morrison's (2005) model as an effective adult learning tool within the practice teacher–student supervisory relationship to guide the student through the learning cycle, whilst trying to balance the four functions of supervision (Management, Educative, Supportive and Mediation). Dunk-West (2013, p.123) highlights the significance of supervision for students as developing social work practitioners – 'Supervision enables students to practise their emerging social work self as well as reflect on this self. Thus supervision is an important place to consider the constitution of the professional self.' Within an educational context the practice teacher supports the students' exploration and analysis of their professional role from initial assessments to endings with service users. The practice teacher is a professional mentor helping the student to test and explore their assumptions, their values and perspectives on working with service users, and promoting reflective practice whereby the student can identify alternative approaches.

The narratives below from the practice teacher and the student give a flavour of the dynamics that exist between and across the range of narratives involved within practice-based learning in social work. The student was placed in a residential setting, working with women and children who have experienced domestic abuse. The practice teacher was independent from the agency and worked off-site. The level of influence each narrative has is dependent on its positioning, requiring exploration of the interaction and interactive aspects within them.

The practice teacher's narrative: part 1

Who am I?

I qualified as a social worker in 2003 and have been a practice teacher for nine years. I am a white Irish female; I live with my partner.

Stage 1: Engagement

During our first supervision session we devised and agreed a contract; this included student and practice teacher expectations, and discussion on the agency's experience and expectations of students. We also discussed the use of self-disclosure and agreed that our supervision would create a 'safe space' in which the student could explore her emotional reactions to the work. We completed the 'Who am I?' exercise as a starting point to acknowledge the power dynamics within our relationship and agreed to use the supervision contract as a learning tool which we would review prior to the midpoint of the placement. Essentially we were agreeing the building blocks of our relationship, agreeing the 'rules of engagement' within our time-limited relationship as practice teacher and student.

In the initial weeks of the practice learning opportunity (PLO) the student completed induction visits and training sessions which enabled her to build relationships with members of the staff team. Within our early supervision sessions the student demonstrated a clear understanding of the agency ethos in terms of self-determination and self-efficacy. We had also discussed her anxiety in relation to allocation of cases. As part of her induction programme the student had participated in house activities with the women and children, cooking meals, doing arts and crafts and having movie nights. This helped the student to gain confidence in her ability to engage with residents and build relationships. The student talked about her feelings hearing some of the women tell their narratives, and the emotional impact it was having for her.

As we were bringing the session to a close the student shared her motivation for wanting to be a social worker – as a child she had experienced living with parental substance misuse. I listened to the student tell her narrative and we worked through this together through a process of interpretation and exploration using dialogue and self-awareness as tools.

The narrative reflects the practice teacher's perspective on the beginning of the practice teacher–student relationship, the 'settling-in phase', contracting the relationship and creating an open environment in which to build and develop trust. This is the Engage stage in the Relationship-Based Model.

The role of attachment in supervision

The use of attachment theory to understand the supervisory relationship is important when trying to make sense of the dynamics occurring between the practice teacher and the student. The student and the practice teacher both bring their own life experiences of attachment to the supervision relationship. Drawing on my own experience as a practice teacher there are key stages in the supervisory relationship when knowledge of attachment theories and styles underpin the dynamics, and parallels can be drawn between the student in the supervisory relationship and the general traits of attachment relationships. Moked and Drach-Zahavy (2016, p.317) concur: 'attachment style is a relatively consistent pattern of expectations, emotions and behaviours in interpersonal situations that develops during infancy, but also affects adults' behaviours in close relationships'. These key stages are the beginning and the end of the practice teacher–student relationship where these dynamics can activate the internal working models of attachment for both the practice teacher and the student (Bennet and Vitale-Saks 2006). For practice teachers this requires modelling their relational skills to provide a 'safe secure base' to facilitate dialogue within a positive learning environment. For students, learning about psychodynamic theories, including attachment, can help to navigate and negotiate the service user's narrative in terms of behaviours and relationships. This enables students to 'make sense' of what is happening in the relationship, and moreover why it is happening, and to come to understand that their intervention may not be enough to affect change in the service user's narrative.

Transformative learning

Social work education is a transformative experience. Brookfield (2006) identified 'personhood' as a significant pedagogic approach in terms of its transformative learning potential. Personhood requires the use of autobiographical examples to illustrate the point the teacher is trying to make to the student. This pedagogic approach affords practice teachers the opportunity to model examples when their viewpoints were challenged and how they learned from the experience. Weld (2012, p.65) comments, 'As supervisors we are not devoid of emotions and nor should we aim to be. Emotions are far too important a source of information for us to try and leave them out of the picture.' The use of self-disclosure by the practice teacher sharing a critical incident from practice is a useful way to model to the student that to disclose personal distress is okay and that in doing so it can help the student to regulate their emotions. Enabling a student to engage in self-reflection is critical to developing their professional identity and recognising their 'professional self'. Grant (2014, p.346) suggests, 'Greater recognition of the potential impact of emotional reactions on self is vital, alongside the development of specific training techniques to enhance reflective abilities, emotional regulation skills and accurate empathy.'

Barriers to achieving this level of openness in the supervisory relationship can exist for both the practice teacher and the student. For the practice teacher there can be a level of unease in relation to exploring emotional responses and feelings with students, being aware of not 'social working' the student. For the student, anxiety of being perceived as stressed out or not coping can create blocks within their learning experience. Without this level of openness and honesty in the supervisory relationship, it becomes difficult to model and build relational trust between the student and practice teacher that can influence the narrative between the student and service user. Harkness (1997, p.43) found a 'causal path from the supervisory skills of empathy and problem solving through the supervisory relationship to direct practice skills'.

The student's narrative: part 1
Who am I?

I am a first placement social work student. I am a white Irish female. I have one child. I returned to study after several years of employment. I am a one-parent family.

Stage 1: Engagement in the supervisory relationship

This was my first placement and my first experience of having a practice teacher and engaging in supervision. I was working in a residential setting with women and children who had experienced domestic violence and abuse. I was apprehensive and unsure what to expect. I was anxious about taking on the role of 'student social worker' and being responsible for service users; would my practice teacher think I was 'good enough' to pass the placement?

After my first supervision session, I felt less stressed. My practice teacher acknowledged my anxieties and we discussed our expectations in terms of the placement and what each of us was bringing to supervision. We discussed our roles and responsibilities and drafted a supervision contract. We talked about what the induction programme would look like over the coming weeks and when I would be allocated my own cases.

In the following weeks I found myself looking forward to supervision and felt supported in my learning. I opened up to my practice teacher and told her about my own experience, my dad and his drinking.

Stage 1: Engagement in the service user relationship

I started working with Ruby in week 5 of the placement. Ruby was a few years older than me with two children. She had been living in the residential setting for three months when I first began working with her. Ruby was known to social services; her children were registered on the child protection register owing to potential concerns of neglect and emotional abuse. Ruby has struggled with substance misuse. I was allocated the case to complete six 1:1 sessions with Ruby with a focus on self-esteem. The work started well: I found it easy to build a rapport with Ruby. I followed the agency guidelines and identified my role as a student social worker and that our work together was time limited. I discussed confidentiality and my role in relation to sharing information in our first session together.

As the weeks progressed we would take a break and have a smoke together outside. This is where I ran into trouble and the boundaries of my relationship with Ruby were tested. I told Ruby I could identify with some of the issues going on in her life. I wanted Ruby to see that I could relate to her.

Question: Why do you think the student wanted to relate to Ruby as 'friends' rather than social worker and service user?

This narrative reflects the student's perspective of her first steps in the engaging stage of building relationships with her practice teacher and one of the women with whom she was working. Communication in social work does not take place in a vacuum: our individual interaction with our own political, social, personal narratives shapes our views of the world, and this makes communication in social work a complex process. In the example, the student is beginning to 'struggle' with managing her relationship with Ruby. She is becoming emotionally involved in Ruby's narrative and this has resulted in the boundaries of their relationship becoming blurred. Ruby and the student were developing different expectations from the relationship. Hingley-Jones and Mandan (2007, p.182) comment, 'The relationship between service user and professional should be both acknowledged and reflected carefully upon as a starting point to inform assessment and intervention.' It is at this point we will return to the student's narrative.

The student's narrative: part 2
Stage 4: (Unplanned) Endings in the service user relationship

I was outside smoking with Ruby when Ruby disclosed that she had been taking her children into town to meet her ex-partner. I was aware from the risk assessment and safety planning meetings that Ruby was required to comply with directions not to have contact with her partner. Any breach of this must be recorded and reported to social services. I knew I had to report this. I also knew that I needed to tell Ruby I was going to report this. But I didn't; I panicked and wanted to get the incident reported as soon as possible. Then I could come and find Ruby and tell her what was happening. Things didn't go according to plan and this had a massive impact on my relationship with Ruby. Social services arrived in the setting within the hour and interviewed Ruby. I tried to speak with Ruby before leaving that evening; she was angry, she told me she thought I was different and she wanted nothing more to do with me or my interfering in her life. This caused the relationship to break down and Ruby refused to engage with me any further throughout the remainder of my placement. It is a steep learning curve from sitting in a lecture listening about how to be a social worker to actually doing the job.

Question: Reflecting on the above what could the student have done differently?

The student attended supervision the following day. Using the Relationship-Based Model as a critical tool to reflect and unpack what happened in the relationship between the student and Ruby, we return to the practice teacher's narrative.

The practice teacher's narrative: part 2
Stage 4: Endings in the student–service user relationship

The student was upset when she arrived for supervision; I made some tea and gave her some space to collect her thoughts. When she felt ready, we discussed what had happened with Ruby the previous day. I asked the student to reflect back to the beginning stage of the relationship. The student recalled a discussion in the kitchen with Ruby and some of the other residents about social workers. The women had shared negative experiences of having social work involvement. She discussed the concept of power and her feelings of discomfort having 'legitimate power' within her professional role. Her discomfort affected the boundaries in the relationship, and she had refrained from revisiting issues of confidentiality and boundaries with Ruby after their initial 1:1 session in week 5 of the practice learning opportunity.

We discussed the student's use of self-disclosure and the impact this had on developing a relationship with Ruby. We talked about the difference between disclosing a personal issue in supervision with a qualified professional supervisor and sharing personal information with a service user. I explored this further with the student: what motivated her to disclose personal details to Ruby? Did she consider how she would feel knowing that Ruby was aware of parts of the student's narrative? Differences exist between intention and perception: the student had intended to convey empathy towards Ruby's narrative; the unknown factor is how Ruby perceived this information. We explored boundaries, the pitfalls of wanting to be liked and over identification with service users. Here the challenge for me was to help the student explore the differences and similarities in their shared narratives whilst acknowledging the impact of over identification which can blur boundaries and create misunderstanding.

I checked with the student if it was okay with her if I shared an example from my own practice which was emotionally charged; I wanted to reassure the student that experiencing personal distress was alright to help her to regulate her emotions and find the learning for practice.

Question: What are your reflections and analysis of the relationship dynamic between the practice teacher and the student? What can you learn from this?

Building resilience

In the example, the student was an active participant in the interactional and intersubjective process of the supervisory relationship with the practice teacher. The 'safe secure space' fostered an open environment in which the student could engage in dialogue and reflection, considering her own narrative and identifying ways to build resilience in emotionally charged situations. Seasoned practitioners are often de-sensitised to the secondary trauma they experience through practice; for students these situations can have a lasting impact. Practice teachers must not lose sight of the impact and influence of our interconnectedness and our environments when exploring the dynamics of relationships. Sedan (2008, p.2) comments, 'Relationship building skills remain the bedrock of quality in practice, especially when people who need a service are anxious, distressed or upset because of the situation.'

These narratives highlight how supervision becomes the central tenet for critical reflection and exploration of the student's relationship with Ruby. The Relationship-Based Model works alongside Kolb's (1984) learning cycle: *Experiencing* (the student tells the story to the practice teacher of what happened with Ruby); *Reflecting* (the student discusses her thoughts and feelings on building and negotiating her relationship with Ruby); *Conceptualising* (the student considers this information and begins making connections with theory to make sense of what happened, the student's actions and Ruby's reaction); and *Experimenting* (the student 'takes' these newly constructed ideas and meaning to apply in her next opportunity to build relationships with service users).

Engagement in critical reflection promotes resilience within social work practitioners alongside the enhancement of their professional identity and practice. In the example, using the Relationship-Based Model as a critical framework within supervision helped the student to develop her relational competence and her ability to critically reflect on the dynamics between her feelings and thoughts, her emotional responses to Ruby and the implications for her future practice. Ingram (2013, p.12) recognises the important role that supervision plays in enabling the practitioner to reflect on 'the functional aspects of their practice but also potentially to critically reflect on the content of their practice'.

The impact of loss and change in the student–service user relationship

Towards the end of the placement I arranged to meet with Ruby to gather her views on how she found the process of working together with the student. Ruby was initially quite negative about the student, commenting, 'We didn't get on, I didn't like her,' as we talked it through. Ruby started saying things like, 'I feel I had no control over what happened; she didn't ask me, she reported me.' Ruby spoke of a previous social worker who had let her down and that she felt her experience with the student was like 'groundhog day'. In this example exploring the issues with Ruby helped her, to some extent, to secure some form of closure; Ruby understood the student was required to report the incident: what hurt Ruby was that the student wasn't open and honest with her.

From the student's perspective she was initially devastated by what happened with Ruby. The experience was a steep learning curve about boundaries and being open and honest with service users, especially around issues of power and control, even more so given Ruby's past experiences of domestic violence and negative experiences of engagement with social workers. The relationship between the practice teacher and student was an essential part of the learning process; supervision provided an opportunity for the student to explore her actions and responses to the change and loss of her relationship with Ruby. The ability of the student to 'cope' with Ruby's rejection, to accept what had happened and why it had happened, enabled the student to be open to unintended insights about herself and others and to develop alternative perspectives on engaging and maintaining relationships with service users.

Conclusion

In this chapter we have explored the practice teacher–student supervisory relationship, looking at the relational dynamics which exist between the practice teacher and student within the supervisory relationship and between the student and service user within the placement setting. Practice teachers provide essential support for students in helping them to understand the complexities and challenges of engaging in relationship-based practice by validating students' experiences, recognising what they bring to the placement, and supervision, and by encouraging students to view their experiences as a starting point for critical reflection.

If we are to encourage students to be open and honest in their relationships with service users, then as practice teachers and mentors we must model this within the supervisory relationship, sharing examples from our own practice, when we have been faced with uncertainty and challenging situations, reflecting on our own practice to demonstrate to students how to reframe relationships and interactions between people.

Reflection points

- Reflect on your own motivation for becoming a social worker; note down your motivations, both intrinsic and extrinsic.

- What tools do you have or have you used to safeguard your wellbeing and your professional development?

- Reflect on some of the relationships within your own life. What characterises a positive relationship? What characterises a negative relationship?

- Have you been in a similar situation to the student or practice teacher in the narratives? What were the dynamics of the situation? What response did you have at that time? What would you do differently if faced with that situation now?

- Think about your own experience of the supervisory relationship as either a practice teacher or student. What helped this relationship to develop? What hindered this relationship?

References

Baldwin, M. (2004) 'Critical Reflection: Opportunities and Threats to Professional Learning and Service Development in Social Work Organisations.' In N. Gould and M. Baldwin (eds) *Social Work, Critical Reflection, and the Learning Organisation.* Aldershot: Ashgate.

Bennet, S. and Vitale-Saks, L. (2006) 'Field notes: a conceptual application of attachment theory and research to the social work student–field instructor supervisory relationship.' *Journal of Social Work Education 42,* 3, 669–682.

Bogo, M. (2015) 'Field education for clinical social work practice: best practices and contemporary challenges.' *Clinical Social Work Journal 43,* 317–324.

Boitel, C. R. and Fromm, L. R. (2014) 'Defining signature pedagogy in social work education: learning theory and the learning contract.' *Journal of Social Work Education 50,* 4, 608–622.

Brodie, I. and Williams, V. (2013) 'Lifting the lid: perspectives on and activity within student supervision.' *Social Work Education 32,* 4, 506–522.

Brookfield, S. D. (2006) 'Authenticity and power.' *New Directions for Adult and Continuing Education 111,* 5–16.

Dunk-West, P. (2013) *How to Be a Social Worker: A Critical Guide for Students.* London: Palgrave Macmillan.

Fook, J. and Gardener, F. (2007) *Practising Critical Reflection: A Resource Handbook.* Milton Keynes: Open University Press.

Ford, K. and Jones, A. (1987) *Student Supervision.* Basingstoke: Macmillan.

Grant, L. (2014) 'Hearts and minds: aspects of empathy and wellbeing in social work students.' *Social Work Education 33,* 3, 338–352.

Handy, C. (1999) *Understanding Organisations.* London: Penguin.

Harkness, D. (1997) 'Testing interactional social work theory: a panel analysis of supervised practice and outcomes.' *Clinical Supervisor 15,* 1, 33–50.

Hingley-Jones, H. and Mandan, P. (2007) 'Getting to the root of the problem: the role of systemic ideas in helping social work students to develop relationship-based practice.' *Journal of Social Work 21*, 2, 171–191.

Ingram, R. (2013) 'Emotions, social work practice and supervision: an uneasy alliance?' *Journal of Social Work Practice 27*, 1, 5–19.

Kolb, D. A. (1984) *Experiential Learning: Experience as the Source of Learning and Development.* Englewood Cliffs, NJ: Prentice Hall.

MacDermott, D. and Campbell, A. (2015) 'An examination of student and provider perceptions of voluntary sector social work placements in Northern Ireland.' *Social Work Education 35*, 1, 31–49.

Mezirow, J. (1990) 'How Critical Reflection Triggers Transformative Learning.' In J. Mezirow and Associates (eds) *Fostering Critical Reflection in Adulthood: A Guide to Transformative and Emancipatory Learning.* San Francisco: Jossey-Bass.

Moked, Z. and Drach-Zahavy, A. (2016) 'Clinical supervision and nursing students' professional competence: support-seeking behaviour and the attachment styles of students and mentors.' *Journal of Advanced Nursing 72*, 2, 316–327.

Morrison, T. (2005) *Staff Supervision in Social Care: Making a Real Difference for Staff and Service Users* (3rd edn). Brighton: Pavillion.

Noble, C. and Irwin, J. (2009) 'Social work supervision: an exploration of the current challenges in a rapidly changing social, economic and political environment.' *Journal of Social Work 9*, 345–357.

Northern Ireland Social Care Council (2009) *The Standards for Practice Learning in Social Work* (revised). Belfast: NISCC.

Northern Ireland Social Care Council (2013) *Readiness to Practise: A Report from a Study of New Social Work Graduates' Preparedness for Practice: An Analysis of the Views of Key Stakeholders.* Belfast: NISCC.

Scholar, H., McLaughlin, H., McCaughan, S. and Coleman, A. (2014) 'Learning to be a social worker in a non-traditional placement: critical reflections on social work, professional identity and social work education in England.' *Social Work Education 33*, 8, 998–1016.

Sedan, J. (2008) *Counselling Skills in Social Work Practice* (2nd edn). Milton Keynes: Open University Press.

Taylor, E. (2007) 'An update of transformative learning theory: a critical review of the empirical research (1999–2005).' *International Journal of Lifelong Education 26*, 2, 173–191.

Urdang, E. (2010) 'Awareness of self – a critical tool.' *Social Work Education 29*, 5, 523–538.

Wayne, J., Bogo, M. and Raskin, M. (2010) 'Field education as the signature pedagogy of social work education.' *Journal of Social Work Education 46*, 327–339.

Weld, N. (2012) *A Practical Guide to Transformative Supervision for the Helping Professionals: Amplifying Insight.* London: Jessica Kingsley Publishers.

Chapter 11

DEVELOPING AND SUSTAINING RELATIONSHIPS IN MULTIDISCIPLINARY WORKING

Mary McColgan

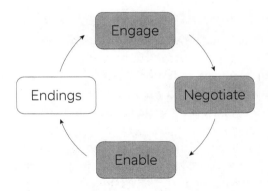

This chapter addresses a number of professional issues related to multidisciplinary working in social work and social care and applies the 4 Stage Relationship Model using an example of working within the context of a case conference.

At the outset, the reader is introduced to some of the dilemmas and the tensions experienced by a range of professionals involved in the complex arena of child and adult safeguarding. Attention is paid to the different definitions of multidisciplinary/interagency/ interdisciplinary working before specific focus is given to exploring the factors which facilitate effective practice in this arena of working and defining models of good practice. The chapter will consider how different models (such as social and medical models which underpin the separate professions involved in safeguarding work) can influence interprofessional working.

Application of the Relationship-Based Model will focus on the three stages of Engage, Negotiate and Enable, identifying the communication skills required to clarify the role and function of the social worker, and to establish effective working relationships with other professionals. Consideration will be given to examining how different professional backgrounds and expectations of each other's professional roles can affect the key area of effective communication between professionals and agencies in safeguarding work. The application of the model will refer to the case scenario in Chapter 3 to illustrate key learning. Finally, the chapter will suggest ways of maintaining relationships, especially where there is conflict or disagreement about the best way to support and meet the needs of the service user.

Definitions of multidisciplinary working

Despite contested definitions and discussion of multidisciplinary working in the literature over many years, the terms 'interdisciplinary', 'multidisciplinary', 'multiprofessional' and 'interagency working' appear to be used interchangeably in the literature. Wilson and Pirrie (2000) suggest that the key issues about definition relate to epistemology, professional boundaries and numbers of staff who work together – arguing that personal commitment, shared purpose and role clarity were the defining features. In seeking to identify the factors influencing multiprofessional working in mental health teams West *et al.* (2012, p.12) found that having the right mix of skills and high levels of team effort alongside a well-defined team task contributed to effectiveness. They also highlight the importance of team leadership and 'practical support for creative and innovative approaches to providing care for services users' and, significantly in teams working with older adults, an absence of team conflict. This emphasis of the combined leadership-cum-interpersonal aspects resonates with earlier work by McGrath (1991) who defined interprofessional working as collegiate practice based on confidence in the expertise of other professionals. The interchangeable usage of the different terms highlights a complex picture which emphasises the resource aspects as well as lack of agreement about what constitutes interagency working and concomitant lack of clarity about which terminology adequately captures the 'working together' engagement between professionals. It is perhaps more relevant to consider how working relationships can be defined. West *et al.* (2012) recommended a priority order of factors underpinned by the cornerstone of clarity about role, purpose and function. The hierarchy of effectiveness is predicated on leadership which values diversity within teams and is reflected in relationships at all levels between team members and service users. Establishing team processes to incorporate clinical review meetings, peer support and appraisal promoted inter-team working with opportunities for reflection.

Frost (2005) expounded a model which conceptualised professional relationships in terms of four levels to partnership working which are predicated on how services are established. He defined the levels as: co-operation, where services worked together but maintained their independence resulting in 'joined up, informal working' (p.15); collaboration, where services were planned together to avoid duplication; co-ordination, where services worked together in a planned approach with agreed goals; and merger or integration, where services were integrated into one organisation to enhance delivery. Collaborative working seemed to emerge as the preferred model of practice as it combined a value-added element of professionals working together for a common purpose but achieving new understanding through this engagement.

Training

Several authors have highlighted the importance of creating opportunities for professionals to train together as the basis for establishing effective working practices. Darlington, Feeney and Rixon (2005) examined some of the factors which either enhance or hinder multidisciplinary practice between child protection service and mental health services, and found that inadequate training was perceived as a major obstacle to effective joint working. The authors concluded that joint training should focus on the attainment of flexible boundaries, dispel interagency myths and challenge negative perceptions of 'others' within multidisciplinary working. This latter aspect of negative perceptions has also been reflected in child abuse and adult safeguarding inquiries where lack of understanding about professional responsibilities has impacted on service users' care and service provision.

There is also evidence to suggest that effective working can emerge through a continuum of training which aims to develop an awareness and application of multidisciplinary working within child protection. Often this can be initiated during undergraduate training, developing awareness of professional roles and values, and is reinforced through cross-discipline initiatives involving more structured and formalised training programmes. Over several decades, the emergence of established and formal interagency training and a drive towards standards for interagency practice (Charles and Glennie 2003; SCIE 2009; Taylor and Daniel 2006) would reflect this development. Unfortunately, the anticipated benefits of formal training in multidisciplinary working – such as the formulation of shared understandings and communication between professionals, enhancing sound decision-making based on information-sharing and increasing understanding of the tasks, roles and responsibilities in shared practice (Brandon *et al.* 2013) – have not been sustained.

Defining models of good practice

Despite the apparent difficulties and complex issues inherent to multidisciplinary practice in child protection services and the resulting impact of the issues on successful outcomes for children and families, it is clear that positive results are precipitated by the collaborative approach. Moran *et al.* (2007) highlight that working within a multidisciplinary environment led to renewed commitment and enthusiasm for the job, fostered a creative approach and increased autonomy in practice. There was also an enhanced understanding of professional roles and modes of working, and an increased confidence in relation to intervention thresholds, both of which enabled partner agencies to make more appropriate and quicker referrals.

Dilemmas and tensions in working in child and adult safeguarding

Hudson (2002) opined that there were three barriers to effective professional engagement:

1. professional identity, which relates to how professionals define their role and themselves

2. professional status, which includes professional hierarchy and power

3. professional accountability, which refers to how professionals manage their daily business.

Combining different organisational contexts adds to the difficulties in co-ordination because specialisation of roles leads to fragmentation of services when professionals are unclear about the contributions of other professionals. Widmark *et al.* (2011) examined barriers to collaboration between heath care, social services and schools and found that the allocation of responsibilities, confidence and professional encounter were areas where barriers occurred but this was mainly due to lack of clarity. Their research suggested that shared responsibility from managers was a key determinant of influencing collaboration between professionals. Thus summarising what promotes good practice in working with other professionals involves attention to:

- clear communication

- time taken to develop communication between members of a team

- developing mutual trust and respect

- joint training initiatives

- clear procedural protocols.

Application of the Relationship-Based Model

Recognising that effective communication is the basis of establishing professional understanding belies the complexity of this process. Misunderstandings can occur because of misperceptions of role, lack of clarity about the legislative mandate of professionals, and differing professional values and perspectives. However, it is not always possible to communicate on a collaborative level as a result of differing communication styles or as a result of communication which remains at the level of basic information-sharing. Devaney (2008) considered interprofessional working in child protection via research conducted with 28 experienced child welfare professionals. The findings underlined a recurring theme of the importance of communication between professionals and between professionals and families. Open and regular communication which incorporated an analysis of the issues in the family and a joint consideration of how to progress the work were highlighted as indicative of sound collaborative practice. Using the Relationship Model at the initial engagement stage would require attention to skills associated with the following tasks:

1. *Tuning in to professional contexts:* This exercise would draw on an understanding of professional roles and activities, for example thinking about the focus of occupational health intervention in adult safeguarding in assessing the risks posed for an older person's activities of daily living: How can they manage in their home environment? To what extent can they be independent in managing tasks such as dressing, cooking, and toileting? And what aids or resources would facilitate the quality of life of the service user and their carers? Developing this knowledge about professional roles and activities will require you to learn about the role of others, the training they have undertaken, the knowledge base they have acquired and the range of skills they can contribute.

2. *Clarifying professional role and function:* As all professional activity is undertaken within a legal and policy framework, it is important to understand these dimensions. As a first step, you will need to think about the legal powers and duties of your own professional group and to reflect on the extent to which these contribute to the 'care and control' aspects of your practice. What are the legal limitations of your role, what are you accountable for and how is this accountability achieved through governance systems in your organisation? Distinguishing the focus of your professional function has to be underpinned by understanding the contested nature and scope of social work. Although there is wide agreement about the value base for social work founded on respect for the inherent dignity of all people, social workers are expected to adopt a holistic perspective – challenging oppression, recognising diversity and promoting human rights, social inclusion and wellbeing of individuals and communities (Asquith, Clark and Waterhouse 2005; International Federation of Social Workers 2014). Explaining these aspects to other professionals is challenging because you

may often need to promote the rights of the service user to self-determination in the face of legitimate professional concerns (in the context of adult safeguarding) or balance proportionate risks in child protection. Thus the skill of clarifying your role and function is based on understanding key aspects such as who you are, what agency you represent and what your particular task is and conveying this understanding in a non-jargonised way. Additional attention to the way in which you convey this understanding, for example the pitch, pace and tone of your voice and accompanying nonverbal expressions, facilitate your communication. An important aspect of developing effective communication at this initial engagement stage involves your ability to convey empathy for the other professionals so the 'tuning in' skill encourages you to see the other person's point of view or to think about the professional perspective of the other person. While examples defining empathy abound in the literature (Egan 2006; Geldard and Geldard 2009; Gerdes and Segal 2011; Lazo and Vik 2014; Shulman 1999; Trevithick 2005) essentially it is about 'seeing the world' from another's perspective. Barker (2003, p.141) defines it as 'the act of perceiving, understanding, experiencing and responding to the emotional state and ideas of another person'. In the context of developing communication skills with other professionals, it means being attuned to and taking account of their verbal and nonverbal communication and recognising that these factors are important in conveying respect for other professional perspectives and facilitating effective communication.

3. *Building rapport with professional colleagues:* This involves establishing common ground and forging professional working through creating bonds of understanding and respect. Although this is often described as 'getting on' with others, the skill combines effective listening, open relaxed body posture, eye contact and a repertoire of topics or ice breakers which are related to social engagement to initiate conversation.

Skills required for the Negotiate stage of the Relationship Model

The ability to achieve consensus or reach a compromise lies at the heart of negotiation skills. In your professional social work role, you may have to bring parties together who have apparent differences or are resistant to reaching agreement on the best way to proceed with an intervention or care plan. Ultimately, setting goals which will reflect how change will be achieved must be based on partnership working and engagement with service users as well as other professionals. Three skills are identified for focus in this section: establishing common ground, assertiveness and dealing with conflict.

Establishing common ground is predicated on your ability to listen to other professional perspectives, to use probing and elaboration questions to fully understand their points of view and to encourage discussion about specific elements. Utilising reflective listening skills, and reframing what you have heard in your own words by making a short statement, convey understanding. Bearing in mind the constraints engendered in working within and across different organisational contexts, it is helpful to take any external factors into account, and agree times and modes of communication. There is also a need to agree a shared language across different professions and roles, so staff can easily understand one another. For example, in working with an older person who experiences dementia, the medical and nursing focus may be on assessing risks associated with activities of daily living, while the social work focus will include a more holistic perspective on social factors, the role of carers as well as the personal views and wishes of the older person and their mental capacity.

Assertiveness skills involve two aspects: (1) having the confidence to put forward your professional point of view in a respectful manner and (2) being able to stand up for the rights of others in a way which is not perceived as being aggressive or argumentative. In many ways it involves a level of self-awareness and self-control about your own reactions and feelings and an ability to respect the feelings and beliefs of others in the responses you make, and conveying values in your written, verbal and nonverbal communication which regard other professionals as equals.

Skills associated with dealing with conflict are the corner stone of professional engagement. Developing effective working relationships combines emotional intelligence with a capacity to use your interpersonal skills to create meaningful relationships where you can challenge professional opinions through conveying your own profession informed by observations, evidence-based practice and research. Understanding that professional conflicts can occur because of different professional perspectives also offers the opportunity to learn from and about the contribution of other disciplines, ultimately enhancing knowledge and information.

Skills required for the Enable stage of the Relationship Model

Many of the skills already identified will apply to the Enable stage of the model. In the context of working with other professionals the focus of intervention is often targeted at achieving some change, whether this involves lifestyle, quality of life, managing identified risks for vulnerable adults and children or minimising the impact of harm. Thus achieving the goals defined in negotiation with service users may require specific input from different professionals if the enable stage is to be progressed as Clarke discussed in Chapter 7, indicating that the enabling stage involves supporting service users to achieve positive change. One of the key messages about how change can be promoted is that challenging resistance to change is often the first task. Ward and Barnes (2016) explore this theme in some detail, positing the view that working in social care transcends an awareness of personal qualities of the professionals involved. In essence, because different professionals are often working together with service users, this dynamic creates a nexus for exploring how their perspectives influence the service users' wellbeing: 'evidence suggests relational rather than individualised practice are most likely to generate well being' (Ward and Barnes 2016, p.908). They acknowledge that for professionals to do this will require a preparedness for working outside the usual comfort zones, connecting their own experiences of the role of care in their own lives with the experiences of service users. In many ways, this challenges power dynamics and suggests that the co-creation of dialogue will enhance the co-production of wellbeing, reminding us that the development of relationship-based practice involves a process.

Case example

In order to illustrate the application of the Relationship-Based Model in practice, the child protection case scenario discussed in Chapter 3 will be used to highlight key aspects. Based on Marshall's preferred pathway for 'child protection relationship-based engagement' the application of the model is considered in the context of a case conference and you are invited to consider and reflect on learning points for engagement, negotiation and enabling stages.

A child protection case conference

A child protection case conference is a meeting which provides a decision-making forum for service user(s) and professionals to share and plan future work. The aim of collating information at a case conference is to reflect on current circumstances, share professional assessments and reports and ensure support and safety to children and families.

This is an opportunity for face to face contact with professionals and service users, and these meetings can be very powerful, evoking strong emotions and differing professional and individual opinions. The outcome of these meetings can have significant impact on relational practice. Service users are not always fully informed or aware of the potential outcomes and this can lead to frustration and mistrust and damage previous positive relationship-building.

The challenge for the social work practitioner is to ensure that in the *Enable stage* they have built a positive working relationship with the service user(s), parents and children prior to and after the meeting has taken place. It is important that the service users are informed and supported prior to the meeting taking place, even though what may be discussed is very difficult to hear or there is a dispute over the possible decisions or outcomes. It is important also that the practitioner is aware of how intimidating and threatening these meetings can appear for service users; for example, it may feel like they are being publicly and openly judged and challenged. Ideally the way in which these meetings are facilitated could change to allow for a less threatening environment.

Referring to the case study explored in Chapter 3, the social worker could explain to Ms B that the information supplied by the school about her son, C, indicates that there are issues about his regular attendance, and the representatives from the school could suggest that this would have implications for his educational attainment as well as his social and emotional development. Ms B may feel that she is being judged on her parenting capacity and ability to care for her son and she may have underlying fears about the outcome of the case conference. Equally the information shared by the GP confirms confidential details about Ms B's health and wellbeing but also raises issues about the immunisation records of her 18-month-old daughter. While the case scenario suggests that the social worker has had to be assertive with the GP in gaining access to these details, the picture which emerges begins to challenge the allegations levelled against Ms B and opens up the possibility of alternative explanations for the original anonymous referral. Thus sharing information about the different professional perspectives could assist the open discussion about the family circumstances and the pressures experienced by Ms B without alienating her in the case conference. It is likely that the professional perspectives would be collated into a report completed by the social worker to be shared with Ms B in advance of the case conference, and the respective professionals would be aware that this was good practice. There are scenarios where sensitive information is not disclosed until the case conference meeting itself and this has the potential to create additional stress for all the participants, especially the service user, so open communication should always be advocated.

Reflection point

Practitioners should be aware that these meetings are very difficult for service users and can often result in service users being very reluctant to engage as they are scared of the outcomes. Professionals need to consider this and explore better ways of engaging and supporting service users to help them contribute to formal meetings. If a number of significant outcomes have been decided this can be difficult for service users as well as practitioners to process. To ensure continued engagement at these significant meetings, the social worker needs to be aware when it is appropriate to offer support and comfort or give the service user time to process the decision. There may be other professionals at the meeting with more expertise or who can give greater clarity, therefore their input and relationship with the service user should be encouraged.

Negotiation at case conference meetings can be both positive and contentious. There can be varying professional opinion in relation to assessment or engagement of the service user(s) or resources/services being offered. In the negotiation stage, at times there can be a professional hierarchy with some professions perhaps assuming greater knowledge or expertise in relation to enabling the decision-making process or assessment. This is the role of the chairperson or facilitator of the meeting: to be fair in the negotiation stage and allow for but also challenge opinion. This is a highly skilled position and often necessitates that this role is undertaken by someone who is regarded as having an unbiased perspective or no direct involvement in the case but from a social work background.

Reflection point

There is a clear power dynamic in a case conference and the chairperson may have the ultimate say in the planning and decision-making process. This power dynamic in terms of negotiation is something that practitioners need to be aware of: how disempowered that service users can feel when someone who does not know them as well appears to make these important decisions in the care of the lives of their children.

Enable stage

Bearing in mind that the sharing of information at a case conference often involves written reports which are circulated for participants to read and individual verbal representations, there is potential for both professionals and service users to feel intimidated and uncertain. Key messages about ensuring everyone's voice and perspective is heard, respected and valued point to the importance of creating a context which encourages open communication.

Sometimes professional jargon can create a barrier to this openness so the written and spoken word needs to be clearly expressed and easy to understand. Weighing up professional judgements has to acknowledge the professional accountability for ensuring that a balanced perspective is conveyed, alongside the professional responsibility for identifying the strengths, areas for development and risks as well as how progress can be achieved and measured. Outlining the different professional perspectives can help to provide a more holistic overview. For example, in Ms B's scenario, the medical confirmation of the updated immunisation would attest to positive parenting aspects. In addition, the confirmation that there is no evidence of addictions or treatment provided would suggest Ms B has shown great resilience in coping with a range of difficulties over a period of time and would reinforce a 'strengths-based' approach to assessing the family situation.

References

Asquith, S., Clark, C. and Waterhouse, L. (2005) *The Role of the Social Worker in the 21st Century – a Literature Review.* Edinburgh: Scottish Executive.

Barker, R. L. (2003) *The Social Work Dictionary* (5th edn). Washington, DC: NASW Press.

Brandon, M., Bailey, S., Belderson, P. and Larsson, B. (2013) *Neglect and Serious Case Reviews.* Norwich: University of East Anglia and NSPCC.

Charles, M. and Glennie, S. (eds) (2003) *Sustaining Quality: Standards for Interagency Child Protection Training and Development* (rev. edn). Leicester: PIAT.

Darlington, Y., Feeney, J. A. and Rixon, K. (2005) 'Interagency collaboration between child protection and mental health services: practices, attitudes and barriers.' *Child Abuse and Neglect 29,* 1085–1098.

Devaney, J. (2008) 'Inter-professional working in child protection with families with long-term and complex needs.' *Child Abuse Review 17,* 4, 242–261.

Egan, G. (2006) *The Skilled Helper: A Problem-Management and Opportunity-Development Approach to Helping* (8th edn). Belmont, CA: Brooks/Cole, Cenage Learning.

Frost, N. (2005) *Professionalism, Partnership and Joined-Up Thinking: A Research Review of Front-Line Working with Children and Families.* Dartington: Research in Practice.

Geldard, K. and Geldard, D. (2009) *Counselling Adolescents: The Proactive Approach for Young People.* London: Sage.

Gerdes, K. E. and Segal, E. (2011) 'Importance of empathy for social work practice: integrating new science.' *Social Work 56,* 2, 141–148.

Hudson, B. (2002) 'Interprofessionality in health and social care: the Achilles heel of partnership?' *Journal of Interprofessional Care 16,* 1, 7–17.

International Federation of Social Workers (2014) *Global Definition of Social Work.* Berne: IFSW.

Lazo, D. and Vik, E. (2014) 'Reflections on Empathy in Social Work Practice: A Qualitative Study among Swedish Social Workers.' Undergraduate thesis, University of Gavle, Sweden.

McGrath, M. (1991) *Multidisciplinary Teamwork.* Aldershot: Avebury.

Moran, P., Jabobs, C., Bunn, A. and Bifulco, A. (2007) 'Multi-agency working: implications for an early-intervention social work team.' *Child and Family Social Work 12,* 143–151.

Social Care Institute for Excellence (2009) *e-Learning: Interprofessional and Interagency Collaboration (IPIAC).* London: SCIE.

Shulman, L. (1999) *The Skills of Helping Individuals, Families, Groups and Communities.* Itasca, IL: F. E. Peacock.

Taylor, J. and Daniel, B. (2006) 'Standards for education and training for interagency working in child protection in the UK.' *Nurse Education Today 26,* 3, 179–182.

Trevithick, P. (2005) *Social Work Skills: A Practice Handbook* (2nd edn). Milton Keynes: Open University Press.

Ward, L. and Barnes, M. (2016) 'Transforming practice with older people through an ethic of care.' *British Journal of Social Work 46*, 4, 906–923.

West, M., Alimo-Melcalfe, B., Dawson, J., El Ansari, W. *et al.* (2012) *Effectiveness of Multi-Professional Team Working (MPTW) in Mental Health Care. Final Report.* NIHR Service Delivery and Organisation Programme. London: HMSO.

Widmark, C., Sabdahl, C., Piuva, K. and Bergman, D. (2011) 'Barriers to collaboration between health care, social services and schools.' *International Journal of Integrated Care 11*, 3.

Wilson, V. and Pirrie, A. (2000) *Multidisciplinary Teamworking: Beyond the Barriers? A Review of the Issues.* SCRE Research Reports 96. Edinburgh: SCRE.

Further reading

Harr, C., Souza, L. and Fairchild, S. (2008) 'International models of hospital interdisciplinary teams for the identification, assessment, and treatment of child abuse.' *Social Work in Health Care 46*, 4, 1–16.

Chapter 12

LOOKING THROUGH THE LENS AT ENDINGS

Service User, Student, Carer and Practice Educator Perspectives on Endings within Social Work Training

Siobhan Wylie and Denise MacDermott

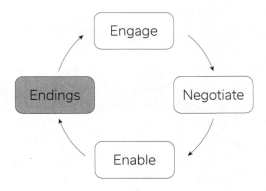

Whilst McMullin focuses on the whole of the relationship, this chapter will look in particular at the ending stage of the Relationship-Based Model, most especially within the context of student social work placement. All relationships must begin somewhere, possibly grow and develop, and lead to separation and ending. Endings are always present in social work practice between social work practitioners and service users. Within social work education and training, endings can represent a real challenge for students who are being assessed, as their 'endings' are determined by the length of the practice learning opportunity and can often have a significant impact on service users, students, practice educators and the staff team.

This chapter will look at the importance of endings within social work professional training, with a focus on the student experience when on placement, as these endings often occur organically as student placements last between 85 and 100 days (Northern Ireland Social Care Council 2009). We learn best through experiential learning (Kolb 1984) so we have included narratives that highlight the very real importance of endings; this will be underpinned with relevant research. There is limited literature available in relation to endings in social work supervision (Gould 1977; Ruch, Turney and Ward 2010; Wall 1994) yet as a practice educator the exploration of endings is central to modelling good social work practice. The quality of the relationship between practice educator and student can often 'mirror' that of the relationship between student and service user. We cannot underestimate the powerful impact that endings with, or disengaging from, a family or service user can engender for all involved.

Understanding the social work relationship

As with all relationships, the ending is influenced by the quality of the relationship which has been established. As the social work profession becomes more entrenched in managerialism and outcome metrics, social work practitioners are spending less contact time with service users, resulting in the impact of loss and endings in social work relationships becoming marginalised. This presents a challenge to students, as developing practitioners, who are encouraged to demonstrate their professional skills on placement, conflicted between actual time spent with families and time spent completing paperwork. 'It is through experiential learning that students develop skills of self-reflection, critical decision making, understanding the theoretical concepts of intervention and demonstrating critical application of knowledge in direct work with service users and carers' (MacDermott and Campbell 2015, p.32).

Within the practice learning context this can be challenging for the practice educator to manage, especially when most endings are governed by the end dates of the placement rather than the service user's needs. However it is clear that this is now being explored in more depth as, in line with the National Occupational Standards (Northern Ireland Social Care Council 2011), the key roles that govern social work and social work training have changed. It is interesting to note that

SW Standard 20 (Key Role 6) gives very clear credence to *disengagement at the end of social work involvement* (Northern Ireland Degree in Social Work Degree Partnership, *Regional Practice Learning Handbook*, 2015, p.155). This has always been integral within themed support training provided by the authors to social work students around endings. At a student support session in April 2016 a number of the students indicated their very real surprise at the impact of ending and disengagement, and how powerful it had been. One in particular said that the impact of her finishing up on placement has engendered powerful feelings not only of loss in one of the individuals that she is working with, but also of powerlessness. The student said that she had felt quite overwhelmed by this and very anxious around the transfer to another support worker in the organisation, which led the practice educator to consider transference, which will be further discussed.

This particular student stated that it was really important that more attention should be given to this at a teaching level, and she would be indicating this within feedback to the university. This has reinforced for the authors the very real importance of signalling endings at the start of the relationship, and indeed ensuring awareness that the *ending* stage of the 4 Stage Relationship Model is every bit as important as the *beginning* stage.

Transference occurs in all human relationships. This is when feelings are 'transferred' from significant relationships in the past to new relationships in the present without consideration of whether they still apply (Clow 2001, p.129). Service users will be allocated a number of social workers over their life course, with each of these experiences influencing the next service user–social worker relationship, based on their experience and expectations. This is thematic throughout the narratives that we have included within this chapter.

For social worker practitioners, students and practice educators, there is a need to understand the difference between healthy 'boundaries-led' professional relationships and loose, unstructured, unclear 'friendships' which can threaten or undermine the safety of all involved. As social work practitioners we must constantly be mindful of our standards of conduct and our professional identity. This is enormously important when we come to the ending stage of the work, and is evident in Jane's narrative below. We have adapted Jane's narrative to the 4 Stage Relationship Model. Drawing on our professional experience as practice educators we can readily identify the value of case studies and narratives as a method of capturing experience as it happened. This equates to an excellent learning tool for others going through a similar situation. Learners always listen when it comes to real life experiences.

Jane's narrative (final-year social work student)

When it was first suggested to me by the team senior that work with one of the families was likely to cease at the next case review meeting, I was in complete disagreement. At this time I had only been working with the family for several weeks and had only begun to build rapport with the family in an effort to gain insight into their dynamics and the complexities of their needs. The thought of ceasing work with the family seemed wrong and unjustified to *me*. I could not comprehend that this family with such a high level of need could possibly be considered ready to manage without *my* support. As I was unable to think of any other justifiable reason for the support service to end, I concluded that this – what seemed to me to be an abrupt and unexpected ending – was the direct result of resource constraints, driven by the agency's need to meet targets.

I decided to speak to a colleague within the team, who was familiar with the family and had worked with them previously. They used informal supervision to give me the opportunity to explore my feelings and express my confusion. Through this she explained the importance of drawing back and ending the support service in order to give families space to put into practice what they have learned throughout the work. By emphasising the importance of giving a family independence and opportunity to function without extra support, she explained how this promotes respect and dignity whilst also giving social services a clearer indication of the family's motivation to change, their capacity to make positive decisions and their genuine willingness to engage.

I began to see the bigger picture; I realised the family had been receiving the intensive support service for an extended period of time and had made good progress in all the identified areas of work. Taking this into account, I began to realise that by focusing on *my agenda, my needs* and *my wants* without considering the family's needs and wishes alongside the work that had been completed with previous workers, I was likely to be having an adverse effect on the family's functioning, creating dependency and delivering unrealistic expectations.

Question: What are your initial thoughts about Jane's reflection on her ending with this family? Discuss.

We will return to Jane's narrative later in the chapter to identify the learning.

Samira's narrative (service user perspective)

Samira had recently arrived in the UK and was in a residential setting.

> The social work student was *my* first point of contact when I arrived here and I developed a very positive and indeed intense working relationship with the student. I felt she gave me the energy and support to move forward in relation to my case. As a female I had suffered immeasurably under *my* own cultural system and then found that I had to fight the system here in the UK. Before I came I thought the UK would be different but this was not the case. The student supported and advocated for me in relation to the injustices that I felt were manifold in terms of my life and access to my children. In *my* view, the student leaving placement added to my stress and anxiety as I knew it would be difficult to move to another key worker, and in an ideal world I would have much preferred to continue working with the student with whom I had an established relationship.

In keeping with an ethical stance and agency policies, the student often raised the fact with Samira that she would be leaving quite soon.

> I found this approach very difficult and said that at times I wanted the student not to remind me that this valued relationship would end without my control.

Despite the fact that the agency acknowledged the difficulties in the transitioning process Samira still found the whole experience extremely challenging, and it took her some time to get used to working with another key worker. There was significant loss and transitioning occurring for her at this time in her life. Samira thought that perhaps if there had been more of a co-working role for a longer period of time, this might have helped her in her experience of endings with the social work student.

> Reflecting on *my* experience of engaging with statutory social services here, I feel that more effort should be put into matching practitioners and service users to achieve a much better working relationship. When the student left there was a big gap – it was a very emotional ending and I felt a very real sense of loss. This was especially so as this student worked so hard to support *me* and she became a pivotal part of my life, when I was experiencing so much change and trauma. However, retelling *my* story to you has made *me* think that there was some merit in the student reminding *me* that this work was time limited. Given the value I placed on *my* relationship with the student, I just didn't want it to end.

This is a clear example of what Thompson (2012, p.79) discusses in relation to loss, 'that the emotional reaction to loss includes sadness, bitterness, resentment, disappointment, anger', clearly underscoring the fact that endings are often very difficult and challenging for service users.

Michael's narrative (carer perspective)

Michael is an only child and the primary carer for his dad, who has mental ill health. The illness impacted on Michael as a four-year-old and this has proved very challenging and often difficult over the years. Michael was in his late teens when he became the primary carer, thus having to meet with social services, who were involved with his father. In terms of endings, this is more a narrative around inconsistent contact with practitioners who come and go within the service (also organisational changes). Clearly, the impact on Michael's father is profound as he is very reluctant to engage with social workers, which obviously has a major effect on Michael, who ultimately is the one with whom the relationship is most developed. Michael has been most impacted by three social work practitioners in the period as primary carer (though there have been others who have come and gone):

1. Michael was nine years old – his father was critically ill and needed hospital admission. A social work practitioner called and Michael's father was very aggressive to her and she could not cope and therefore terminated the meeting and was never seen again (she did not even follow up) – this had a very negative impact on the family.

2. Michael is now the primary carer. His father is living alone with support from the Mental Health Team. The social work practitioner was exceptionally good, and took a real interest in the father and his interests and worked well around this. In engaging via interests and hobbies, the social work practitioner used innovative methods to build a relationship. In terms of Michael, the social work practitioner kept him in the loop and updated him continuously and ensured he got support also. This made such a difference to Michael as a carer, and to his father in terms of managing his own life. The social work practitioner and the family worked together for two years. Due to cuts and team reorganisation, this social work practitioner had to disengage – he was very clear on the reasons for this and it was done in a professional, yet human, down-to-earth way, which made the ending a bit less stressful. Michael believes his father really misses working with this social work practitioner but would not admit it. Michael really misses him too and he also made a very positive ending with Michael and emphasised how much he enjoyed working with Michael's father, which was very helpful for Michael. The social work practitioner ensured that he also met Michael to make a proper ending.

3. Currently, Michael and his father have another social work practitioner and this relationship is not brilliant because there is no contact. Michael thinks that the reason they are not involved is because his father is managing reasonably okay; however, Michael met with the social work practitioner once and it was to tell them basic information that should have been known – this was most frustrating for Michael. The social work practitioner may have tried to contact his father, but Michael is not sure about this and, anyway, he knows that his father would be reluctant to engage.

The practice educator's narrative

It would be remiss to discuss the student experience without mentioning one of the authors' narratives that occurred as a student on placement. My final placement was working with older people who had some form of dementia. One case involved intense work with the spouse of a man who had Alzheimer's, who will be known as Smith. The couple had come home to retire and Mrs Smith was not from the UK and found adapting to life here quite difficult. They had no children and support was fairly limited. This placement was at a time when service users (or clients as they were known) were visited on a weekly basis. Ostensibly this was to engage with Mr Smith; however, more often than not, it was emotional support for Mrs Smith – agreed by the supervisor to be a pivotal part of the work. At the outset student status was declared and the fact that this would be a piece of work that would last over 3–4 months. At approximately mid-point of the work I raised the fact that I would be leaving and handing over the case in a matter of weeks. Mrs Smith became quite distressed and asked would I please continue to visit even when the placement had ended – briefly I was tempted. However, I recognised that this would be completely unprofessional and had to explain this and indeed revisit boundaries for both myself and Mrs Smith. I did some reading around endings prior to the final visit; however, this did not prepare me for the impact of this when it happened. The final visit was arranged for the last week of placement and it was clear from the start that Mrs Smith was reluctant to complete the work, and it was not deemed necessary to hand this particular case over to another member of the team. It was felt that things were quite well contained and managed within this case; in other words it was not a priority case. The visit was handled in a professional manner, and, whilst Mrs Smith did state that she wished that I was continuing to work with her for a longer period, goodbyes were made with both; Mrs Smith accompanied her to the door and became a little tearful. It felt appropriate to hug as we said goodbye.

Unpacking the learning about endings
Jane (social work student)

As Jane began preparing to end her direct work with the family, she became increasingly aware of the challenges and ethical dilemmas that were likely to arise. In order to prepare for this phase Jane read around the endings phase of direct work with service users in order to 'tune in' and gain insight of the complexities of this process. Literature by Ford and Jones (1987) and Ellery (2012) helped to broaden her understanding of what the potential thoughts and feelings of the service users might be, as well as her own, and enabled Jane to prepare herself for an effective and meaningful ending phase. She commented:

> From this piece of work I have learned that closure becomes a more natural process if it is dealt with throughout. This is something I will aim to do through open communication and honesty in all my future work.

Samira (service user)

The impact of time-limited placements negatively affected Samira's experience working with the social work student. Transference from previous relationships within Samira's own narratives and the endemic sense of loss she continues to experience suggest that Samira requires further support from within the agency to process these experiences. In this example the perspectives of the student social worker and Samira differ in terms of the ending outcome. As a result this requires further exploration by the new practitioner to minimise the impact of 'unfinished business' within her working relationship with Samira.

Michael (carer)

The qualities that Michael perceived as important in his narrative with the second social work practitioner around endings was the positive way in which it was done, and this was instrumental in preparing his father and Michael for their relationship with the practitioner to end. Clow (2001, p.137) supports this view, 'An ending that is carefully and thoughtfully managed will improve the degree to which gains from the work are internalised and maintained.' Michael very much credits his father's reasonable quality of life to this social work practitioner. Indeed, prior to this practitioner working with Michael's father, his psychiatrist was convinced that he would not function in the community – and yet he still is today.

Practice educator

Reflecting on my own experience as a student, I became very upset on the drive back to the office and had to pull over. I was mostly not expecting the impact of this to be so powerful, and had to work hard to process this myself as I felt discussing this in supervision would be a sign of weakness. There were a number of very powerful feelings that this ending engendered, and the learning within this for me was that I would ensure that I would take care around future endings within my work and be much more prepared for the impact on both service user and worker.

The challenge was managing very powerful emotions and trying to regulate these feelings without the support of my practice educator, as I viewed this as a sign of weakness and an attribute which might compromise my placement and professional training. Solomon (2010, p.145) comments, 'Some social workers have come to defend themselves against the powerful feelings stirred up by their work.' This experience taught me the significance of exploring my feelings and being open and responsive to the use of self. 'Often there is a sense of loss and separation in both the professional and the service user when a relationship comes to an end' (Lombard 2010). Huntley (2008, p.59) posits that the impact of a negative ending in a practitioner–service-user relationship may undo much of the positive work that has been achieved. When we consider the 4 Stage Relationship Model, and look at the first three stages and the importance of these in the relationship-building process, we can recognise that a badly handled ending could sabotage all that has gone before (Wilson *et al.* 2008, p.15) and would clearly be a very negative experience for both practitioner and service user, and this has been touched upon within some of the narratives.

Jane

Jane's narrative highlights the inner struggle that she endured at the thought of disengaging from the work with this family; however, it does show that careful preparation for the ending can lead to a reasonably positive outcome for all involved. This piece of work chimes with the views of Solomon (2010) when she states that if possible we should help service users (and, we would also propose, practitioners) use the experience of ending in our work in a way that will support them in the future – as with the second practitioner in Michael's narrative, where his father is today still able to function on his own.

Samira

Samira's narrative teaches us the very real importance of being culturally aware, so that we can better understand how to adapt the Relationship Model within this, and also how loss of identity, culture and country can further impact on endings within this situation. It is vital that practitioners become much more culturally adept and that this is taught within the degree curriculum.

Michael

Even though Michael's negative interaction with the first practitioner happened some time ago, it is obvious that he is still impacted by the experience. Howe (2009) discusses the importance of attachment within relationship-based work, and in particular the negative experiences that many people have over the course of their lives; in Michael's case we see that as a nine-year-old he is confronted with a mentally unwell parent, who may have been a pivotal attachment figure. He then is confronted with the 'professional' who cannot cope with the situation – this was clearly a negative experience for Michael. This underscores the premise that the social work practitioner's own reactions and responses to service users and their families are of central importance, as they can significantly affect the quality of the casework.

Practice educator

In relation to the practice educator's narrative, there was clearly an unresolved attachment issue going on and this resonates with Solomon's assertion that 'social workers have issues with endings too' (cited in Ruch *et al.* 2010, p.178). These issues must be acknowledged and explored within the context of professional supervision, recognising that knowledge of self is pivotal in how we deal with the feelings engendered by endings and separation. As practitioners, when we acknowledge our own feelings towards loss, separations and endings, we gain a better insight into the concept of endings for service users.

Jane's ending with the family in her narrative below highlights an example of a well thought-out and planned disengagement incorporating a ritual to mark the ending of the work with the child in the family.

Upon reflection I have concluded that endings should be based on a mutual sense of closure. Fortunately I was able to use the two-week phase-out period to negotiate and empower the family to recognise their own strengths. This meant that by the time of our last visit the primary carer was able to express that he felt ready for closure. However, had this case closed abruptly after the case review this would not have been the case. For me this has highlighted the importance of working in partnership to ensure service users are central to decision-making and have a genuine say in whether they feel ready or not.

The two-week phase-out also provided opportunity to review our progress and discuss the next steps for the family after the service terminated. By completing a final review via our assessment tool, they were able to see clearly the progress that had been made. Evaluating the work in this way helped them to recognise strengths and future areas of progression. I also planned an art and craft activity to do with the child so that she would have something to remind her of the work we completed and the time we had spent together.

I do believe that the ending was positive. I had the opportunity to talk to all three members of the family and explain why the service was ceasing. By doing this in a way that was encouraging and which reflected the good progress they had made, I think I displayed hope, showed respect and empowered the family members. Before I left, the primary carer thanked me for the work I had done with them and joked about the freedom he was now going to have. The youngest child thanked me, gave me a hug and said she would miss me. These gestures provoked mixed emotions within me but through good supervision with my practice educator I was able to reflect and explore my own emotions.

As the narratives in this chapter have illustrated, endings in relationships are challenging and can be difficult for all of those involved in the process, even when the work has ended satisfactorily. Encouraging service users to express their feelings about endings can act as a relational tool in helping service users move on from past losses and endings which were never fully reconciled. The way in which endings are communicated and the messages received dominate our feelings and responses and can evoke powerful emotions of loss, denial, anger, rejection and resolution (Shulman 2015). Given the subjective nature of human relationships we must aspire to achieve what Winnicott (1964) referred to as 'good enough endings'.

It is also important to consider the 'ultimate' ending when either the service user or indeed the practitioner dies, and how this can be worked through. Losing a service user to death can be extremely difficult, most particularly if it is suicide. Currer (2008, p.33) alludes to suicide as an individual act. However, the consequence can impact exponentially for all of those involved, and many practitioners experience this, and are left wondering what they could have done differently or better, or how they missed the signs. Robust supervision alongside team and peer support is vital at this time if the practitioner is to support those most affected by the suicide. This pertains to all forms of loss through death, within both social work itself and social work training the right form of support is vital. Practitioners may even need to avail themselves of staff care at this time, and should not be afraid to ask for help and support – *this is not a sign of weakness*. Losing a member of the team can also be extremely traumatic and should be dealt with in a professional and compassionate manner. The important aspect to note here is that asking for the right help should enable those involved to work through the loss in an appropriate and safe way.

Conclusion

In this chapter we have discussed the narratives of service users, carers and social work students, and it is obvious from this that endings are a hugely pivotal part of the Relationship-Based Model. There are many challenging issues that are raised within this, not least the lack of emphasis on this for students within their training. Our practice learning centre's themed support workshop on endings always engenders a real sense of understanding for students on the vital importance of a well-managed or 'good enough' ending and the impact thereof. In many cases service users have experienced multiple endings with a range of allied health professionals. If we want to achieve positive outcomes for individuals whose lives can often be complex and messy, we must pay more attention to the ending phase of the work, especially where a lot of effort and time have gone into building a relationship. The authors propose that the 'ending stage' of the 4 Stage Relationship Model is vastly important, and holds as much prominence as all of the other stages. We also propose that much more attention and focus – both within education and practice – be given to endings.

Reflection points on Endings in social work training

- *Preparation:* This is essential. Endings alongside an acknowledgement of the time-limited nature of the work must be included in the engaging stage of building a relationship with service users. It is necessary to be clear on each other's roles and expectations; this affords service users the opportunity to make an informed decision on whether or not they wish to work with a student social worker.

- *Role play:* The use of role play can help to develop practitioners' observational and critical reflection skills. This can be completed in supervision with the practice educator/supervisor taking the role of the service user, enabling the supervisee to identify alternative approaches and consider how to manage rejection by the service user and consider their responses to 'boundary testing' within relationships.

- *Focus on feelings:* Use opportunities in supervision to discuss loss and change processes; explore your own responses to loss, reflecting on past experiences and integrating theory and current practice to see the 'bigger picture'.

- *Minimise dependency:* Build in time within the relationship to revisit and phase in the ending stage. Move to fortnightly or monthly contact as a planned rehearsal. This can help the practitioner gain an understanding of the service users' ability to manage change in terms of the level of professional contact.

- *Work through unfinished business:* Ensure that the work that you set out to do with the service user is completed, if this is possible. Keep a focus on this and a momentum so that both practitioner and service user feel that they are achieving something through the engagement. However, it is important to note that service users sometimes begin to disengage early or even sabotage the relationship. It is vital to be mindful of this and try to remain focused on any unfinished work. If the case is to be handed over make sure that the new practitioner is introduced (where possible) to the service user and that they are clear on what has been worked through and what is still to be achieved – Samira's points should be remembered at this stage.

– *The importance of a 'ritualised ending' by way of celebrating the work completed:* It can often be beneficial to have a 'ritual' to mark the ending of the work, as we saw in Jane's narrative. Quite often rituals mark particular change or transitions in the life cycle, often referred to a 'rites of passage' (Currer 2008, p.41). Rituals in themselves are any formal actions following a set pattern which can be expressed through something symbolic or a shared activity that is important to those involved. This, if done carefully, could support a well-thought-through and satisfactory ending.

References

Clow, C. (2001) 'Managing Endings in Practice Teaching.' In H. Lawson (ed.) *Practice Teaching – Changing Social Work*. London: Jessica Kingsley Publishers.

Currer C. (2008) *Loss and Social Work*. Exeter: Learning Matters.

Ellery, A. (2012) 'Ending in Social Care.' Available at https://andyellery.wordpress.com/2012/04/27/endings-in-social-care-adapted-from-m-protected-post-for-first-years-at-the-university -of-central-lancashire, accessed on 8 March 2016.

Ford, K. and Jones, A. (1987) *Student Supervision: Practical Social Work Series*. London: Macmillan Education.

Gould, R. (1977) 'Students' experience with the termination phase of individual treatment.' *Smith College Studies in Social Work 48*, 235–269.

Howe, D. (2009) *A Brief Introduction to Social Work Theory*. London: Palgrave Macmillan.

Huntley, D. (2008) 'Relationship-based social work – how do endings impact on the client?' *Practice 14*, 2, 59–66.

Kolb, D. A. (1984) *Experiential Learning: Experience as the Source of Learning and Development*. Englewood Cliffs, NJ: Prentice Hall.

Lombard, D. (2010) 'How to say goodbye.' *Community Care Magazine*, 28 October.

MacDermott, D. and Campbell, A. (2015) 'An examination of student and provider perceptions of voluntary sector social work placements in Northern Ireland.' *Social Work Education 35*, 1, 31–49.

Northern Ireland Degree in Social Work Degree Partnership (2015) *The Regional Practice Learning Handbook*. Belfast: NISCC.

Northern Ireland Social Care Council (2009) *The Standards for Practice Learning for the Degree in Social Work*. Belfast: NISCC.

Northern Ireland Social Care Council (2011) *National Occupational Standards for Social Work*. Belfast: NISCC.

Ruch, G., Turney, D. and Ward, A. (eds) (2010) *Relationship-Based Social Work: Getting to the Heart of Practice*. London: Jessica Kingsley Publishers.

Shulman, L. (2015) *The Skills of Helping Individuals, Families, Groups and Communities* (8th edn). Belmont, CA: Wadsworth/Thomson Learning.

Solomon, R. (2010) 'Working with Endings in Relationship-Based Practice.' In G. Ruch, D. Turney and A. Ward (eds) *Relationship-Based Social Work: Getting to the Heart of Practice*. London: Jessica Kingsley Publishers.

Thompson, N. (2012) *Grief and Its Challenges*. London: Palgrave Macmillan.

Wall, J. (1994) 'Teaching termination to trainees through parallel processes in supervision.' *The Clinical Supervisor 12*, 2, 27–37.

Wilson, K., Ruch, G., Lymbery, M. and Cooper, A. (2008) *Social Work: An Introduction to Contemporary Practice*. London: Pearson Education.

Winnicott, D. W. (1964) *The Child, the Family and the Outside World*. London: Penguin Books.

AUTHOR BIOGRAPHIES

Julia Alexander currently works for Headway East London, managing the community support work service. The organisation works with survivors of brain injury. Prior to 2016, Julia worked as a regional manager for seven years with Le Chéile Mentoring and Youth Justice Support Services in the Republic of Ireland. Since qualifying as a social worker in 2001 from the University of Dundee, Julia has held several posts in the area of youth justice in charities and local authorities across the UK and Ireland. She holds qualifications in management, supervision and reflective practice and secondary teaching.

Geraldine Campbell has been a lay council member of the Northern Ireland Social Care Council since 2007. During this time she has been instrumental in the development of the role of service users and carers in the decision-making of the regulation of the social care workforce in Northern Ireland. Geraldine has a background in the development of policy, models and practices in promoting partnership working between organisations and the people most affected by the decisions an organisation makes. She has a particular interest in the regulation of professional workforces in the UK and has been influential in ensuring the service user/patient voice is heard and respected in this arena.

Stephen Clarke is a trainee clinical psychologist and completed a psychology degree at Queen's University Belfast in 2000 before working in a number of mental health roles in Belfast and Derry. In 2014 he completed an MSc in Applied Psychology (Mental Health and Psychological Therapies) at Ulster University, where his research focused on the mental health of adolescents who had accessed a postvention programme in response to bereavement and loss, presenting the findings at the Irish Association of Suicidology's 2014 conference. Stephen then completed two assistant psychologist roles, one in a service for individuals with intellectual disabilities, and the other in a paediatric psychology service, before returning to Queen's University Belfast in September 2016 to commence clinical training in the Doctorate in Clinical Psychology.

Dr Lynn Connor is a consultant clinical psychologist employed in the Western Health and Social Care Trust's (WHSCT) Therapeutic Service for Looked After Children. Dr Connor has worked within the setting of looked after children for the past 14 years. Most recently she has been awarded her accreditation as a practitioner in dyadic developmental psychotherapy. Over the past eight years Dr Connor has assisted her colleagues and co-authors Dr Adrian McKinney and Mr Paul Harvey in the development and implementation of MAP within residential care, foster care and services for children with disability.

Mr Paul Harvey has worked within social care for over 30 years from early years provision to child protection; however, his main interest has been in residential childcare. He has worked as a residential social worker, residential social work manager and service manager, and has now been in his current position as the Model of Attachment Practice project lead for four years. He is committed to promoting attachment-based practice through his involvement in the development of Irish Attachment in Action, an affiliate of Scottish Attachment in Action, of which he has been a member for some years. He is also an independent trainer on 'Attachment-Based Practice and Development'.

Mary Henihan is currently the regional manager with Le Chéile Mentoring and Youth Justice Support Services in the Republic of Ireland. This role involves managing a team of mentor coordinators and project staff who co-ordinate regional mentoring and restorative justice projects in the south and midland areas of Ireland. As part of the management team Mary's role extends to the strategic management and effective service delivery of the organisation. She has vast experience of working within the youth justice sector, working with agencies within the community, voluntary and statutory sectors. Mary obtained her master's in social work from University College Cork. She also has a higher diploma in youth and community work from the National University College Maynooth and a BA in humanities, majoring in sociology and psychology, graduating from the University of Limerick. Mary has worked in the field of youth work and community work for the past 12 years. Since 2010 her main area of work and expertise has been in the field of youth justice and restorative justice, and she is a validated trainer of trainers with the International Institute of Restorative Practices. Previous posts include youth services co-ordinator of the Northside Family Resource Centre in Limerick City – co-ordinating and managing youth services for at-risk young people based in the regeneration areas of the Northside of Limerick City.

Brenda Horgan is a professional adviser with responsibility for the Participation Partnership. Originally qualified as a social worker she now works within the workforce development team at the Northern Ireland Social Care Council.

Denise MacDermott works at Ulster University where she is course director for the undergraduate social work degree programme and teaches on the post-qualifying practice teacher programme. Denise is a qualified social worker and has extensive experience of supervising staff and students. She is also a practice teacher, assessor and professional supervisor.

James Marshall is an associate lecturer at Ulster University and he also practises as an independent social worker. His professional family and child practice experience has been with statutory social services and the NSPCC. His research interests and publications include child protection decision-making, risk assessment and ABE (Achieving Best Evidence) interviewing of children for court.

Susannah McCall is currently faculty partnership manager (Faculty of Social Sciences), social work practice learning co-ordinator and a social work lecturer at Ulster University.

Professor Mary McColgan OBE is head of the School of Sociology and Applied Social Studies and head of Social Work at Ulster University. She has an extensive professional background in social work education and has supervised students involved in qualifying and post-qualifying social work and PhD programmes. She also holds a practice teaching qualification and co-authored three child development apps through the Northern Ireland Social Care Council (NISCC).

Uel McIlveen has been a member of the NISCC Participation Partnership for seven years, is an expert with lived experience and comes from a mental health recovery background.

Dr Adrian McKinney is the clinical director of psychology in the Western Health and Social Care Trust (WHSCT) and consultant lead clinical psychologist for the WHSCT Therapeutic Service for Looked After Children. After 15 years of working in CAMHS Dr McKinney took up his present post with the Therapeutic Service, where he has focused his clinical work for the last 11 years and where, along with his colleague Mr Paul Harvey, he began the process of developing a therapeutic approach to working within residential childcare. Dr McKinney is also an accredited practitioner in dyadic developmental psychotherapy.

John McLaughlin was a social work lecturer at Ulster University, Northern Ireland, working with social work degree students and on post-qualifying programmes. Prior to this he was a social work lecturer at Queens University, Belfast. John's interests were in the areas of adult services, health care in social work, disability, ethics and community-based social work. Prior to his teaching posts John was a hospital social worker (team leader) and a development and training officer with social services in Belfast.

Cheryl McMullin is currently the practice learning centre manager in Bryson Care, Northern Ireland, which supports and provides social work placements for degree students. After qualifying in 2002 with her degree in social work from Robert Gordon University, Aberdeen, she moved to Northern Ireland, gaining extensive experience within family and childcare, looked after children and youth offending. During this time she became a qualified practice teacher/educator and moved into training and development in the voluntary sector in 2013. After successfully completing an MSc in Professional Development in Social Work from Ulster University in 2014 she is now studying at Queen's University Belfast for a doctorate in childhood studies.

Maria Somerville is a member of the NISCC Participation Partnership. She is a parent and carer of a disabled son with a rare genetic disorder.

E. James Todd is a social work training and development consultant with the Southern Health and Social Care Trust in Northern Ireland. He has 20 years of experience in rehabilitation and social work practice within the social care sector as a practitioner, manager and educator. Interests include the needs of older people in the community, adult safeguarding/protection and statutory mental health assessment.

Siobhan Wylie BA, MSW has been involved in social work for over 20 years and has a background of working with older people, families and children; she has also worked for over ten years with Relate as a counsellor. She has been engaged in practice education since 2003, and has run the practice learning centre in Bryson Care (Voluntary Sector) in Belfast since 2008. Siobhan has been involved in research within the field of advocacy and learning disability, and she is a passionate advocate for the promulgation of relationship-based social work within the voluntary sector.

SUBJECT INDEX

AUTHOR INDEX

DATE DUE	RETURNED